WORKS SUITE 2000

in easy

STEPHEN COPESTAKE

COMPUTER
STEP

In easy steps is an imprint of Computer Step
Southfield Road . Southam
Warwickshire CV47 OFB . England

http://www.ineasysteps.com

Notice of Liability

Every effort has been made to ensure that this book contains accurate
and current information. However, Computer Step and the author shall
not be liable for any loss or damage suffered by readers as a result of
any information contained herein.

Trademarks

Microsoft® and Windows® are registered trademarks of Microsoft
Corporation. All other trademarks are acknowledged as belonging to
their respective companies.

Printed and bound in the United Kingdom

ISBN 1-84078-113-0

Contents

The Database

4

149

The Calendar

191

5

Home Publishing 2000

197

6

A common approach

This chapter shows you how to get started quickly in any Works 2000 module. You'll learn how to create new documents (where appropriate) and how to open/save existing ones. Finally, you'll learn how to send Works Suite 2000 documents as email attachments, directly from within Works itself.

Covers

Chapter One

Introduction

In this book, the term 'principal modules' always refers to Word, the Spreadsheet and Database modules and the Calendar.

Works Suite 2000 consists of four principal modules:

- Word

- The Spreadsheet

- The Database

- The Calendar

In addition, there are five additional modules:

— Encarta Interactive World Atlas

— Home Publishing 2000

— Picture It! Express 2000

— AutoRoute Express Europe

— Money 2000 Standard

If you're using Works 2000 instead of Works Suite 2000, you won't have access to Word. Instead, the native Word Processor module will be installed.

(For how to use the Word Processor module, see 'Works 2000 in easy steps'.)

The illustration below shows Word's opening screen. Flagged are components which are common to the other principal modules, too (except Calendar).

Toolbar contents vary somewhat from module to module.

The ruler is only present in Word, Home Publishing 2000 and Picture It! Express.

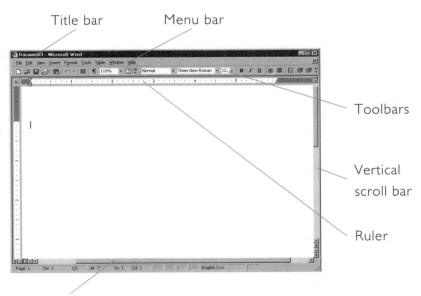

Title bar   Menu bar

Toolbars

Vertical scroll bar

Ruler

Horizontal scroll bar

...cont'd

Compare the Word screen on the facing page with the following:

The Calendar's screen is rather different – see Chapter 5.

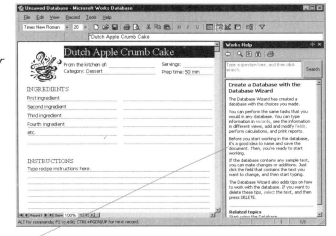

Database screen

This is the Works HELP screen – see the relevant topics in chapters 3-4 for how to use it.

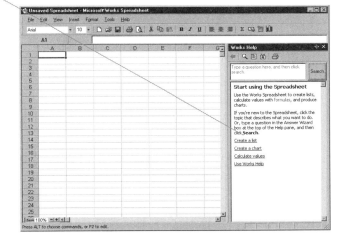

Spreadsheet screen

There are, of course, differences between the module screens; we'll explore these in later chapters.

Notice that many of the screen components are held in common. The purpose of this shared approach is to ensure that users of Works Suite 2000 can move between modules (especially the principal ones) with the minimum of readjustment.

Compare the earlier screens with these:

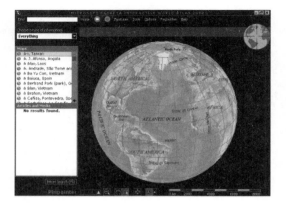

Encarta
Interactive
World Atlas

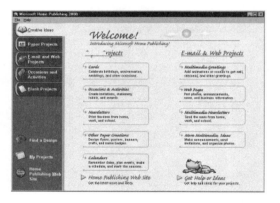

Home
Publishing
2000

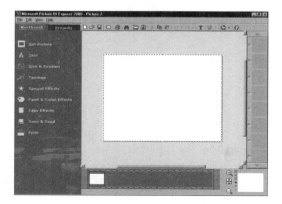

Picture It!
Express
2000

And these:

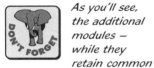

As you'll see, the additional modules — while they retain common features such as menu bars and often toolbars — are more individualistic.

(However, they can all be launched from within the Works Task Launcher.)

AutoRoute
Express
2000

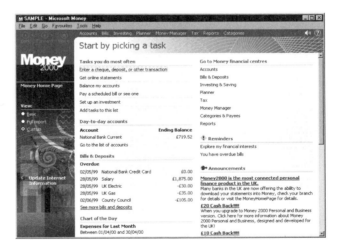

Money
2000
Standard

For how to work with the screens on this and the facing page, see the relevant chapters.

The Works Suite 2000 toolbars

Toolbars are an important component in the principal Works Suite 2000 modules, and in some of the additional ones. A toolbar is an on-screen bar which contains shortcut buttons. These symbolise (and allow easy access to) often used commands which would normally have to be invoked via one or more menus.

In the Spreadsheet, Database, Calendar, Home Publishing 2000 and Picture It! Express modules, there is only one available toolbar. (In Encarta World Atlas and Money there are none.)

For example, Word's Standard and Formatting toolbars let you:

• create, open, save and print documents

• perform copy-and-paste and cut-and-paste operations

• align, embolden, italicise or underline text

• apply a new typeface and/or type size to text

• spell- and grammar-check text

• send documents as email attachments

by simply clicking on the relevant button.

Toolbars vary from module to module.

Hiding/revealing toolbars in Word

Pull down the View menu and do the following:

Re step 2 – the tick signifies that a toolbar is currently visible.

Click here

2 Click a toolbar

Hiding/revealing toolbars in the Spreadsheet and Database modules

 To show or hide the toolbar in Picture It! Express, follow step 1 on the right.

Pull down the View menu and do the following:

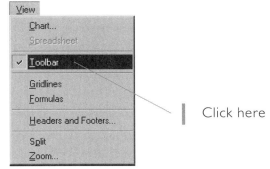

Click here

 AutoRoute Express Europe 2000 has four toolbars. These are:

- *Standard*
- *Mapping*
- *Drawing, and;*
- *Text Labels*

To show or hide any of these, pull down the View menu and click Toolbars. In the sub-menu, click a toolbar.

Hiding/revealing toolbars in the Calendar module

Pull down the View menu and do the following:

Click Toolbar

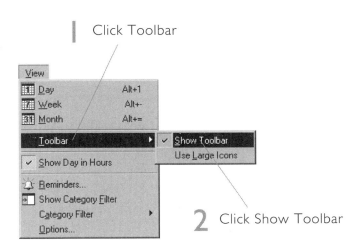

2 Click Show Toolbar

 You can't hide the toolbar in Home Publishing 2000.

New document creation

The following modules – by their very nature – do not let you create new documents:

- *Calendar*
- *AutoRoute Express*
- *Encarta World Atlas, and;*
- *Money 2000*

However, Money 2000 lets you create accounts while in AutoRoute Express you can save calculated routes as files. (See chapters 8 and 9 respectively.)

Some of the additional modules – Home Publishing 2000 and Picture It! Express – also let you create new documents from templates, though the procedure is different.

Most of the principal Works Suite 2000 modules let you:

- create new blank documents

- create new documents with the help of a 'Wizard'

- create new documents based on a 'template' you've created yourself

Creating blank documents is the simplest route to new document creation; use this if you want to define the document components yourself from scratch. This is often not the most efficient way to create new documents.

Wizards are a shortcut to the creation of new documents. You work through one or more dialogs (usually one), answering the appropriate questions and making the relevant choices. Wizards greatly simplify and speed up the creation of new documents while at the same time producing highly professional results.

Templates are sample documents complete with the relevant formatting and/or text. When you've created and formatted a document (so that it meets your requirements) you can save it to disk as a template. Basing a new document on this template automatically provides access to any inherent text and/or formatting, a great timesaver.

Documents created with the use of Wizards or templates can easily be amended subsequently.

All three document creation methods involve launching the Works Suite 2000 Task Launcher. This is a useful Internet-style screen which you can also use to open existing Works documents

For more information on opening Works documents, see pages 21-22.

Creating blank documents

To launch the Task Launcher from within Word, pull down the File menu and click New, Works Task Launcher.

You can create a new blank document from within any of the Works Suite 2000 modules (except Calendar, AutoRoute Express, Encarta World Atlas and Money 2000).

The first step is to launch the Task Launcher. From within any principal module except Word and Calendar, pull down the File menu and click New. Now carry out the following steps:

To view the Task Launcher from within Calendar or any of the non-principal modules, hold down Alt then press Tab until the Launcher's icon:

is visible in the on-screen bar. When it is, release Alt.
(This technique assumes the Launcher has already been run. If it hasn't, first click the Windows Start button. Select Programs, Microsoft Works.)

1 Click Programs

2 Click the relevant module entry

3 Click here

If you've selected Works Database in step 2 (to create a new blank database), Works Suite 2000 doesn't immediately comply after step 3; before it can do so, you need to define the necessary fields.
(See page 151 for how to do this.)

4 In the case of non-principal modules, carry out the additional steps on page 16, as appropriate

Additional steps

Perform one of the following additional procedures, as appropriate:

If you want to create a new blank document immediately after you've started Works Suite 2000, you don't need to launch the Task Launcher manually: it appears automatically.

Once the Task Launcher is on-screen, however, you can follow the appropriate steps on this and the facing page to produce the relevant blank document.

5 In Home Publishing 2000, pull down the File menu and click New, Blank Paper Project. In the Themes box, select a theme. In the main part of the screen, double-click a design e.g.:

5 In Picture It! Express 2000, do the following:

After step 5 in Picture It! Express 2000, use the Command bar on the left of the screen to set:

- *the page orientation, and;*
- *the page proportions*

  Finally, click Done.

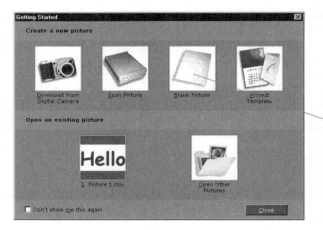

Click here

For how to create a new account in Money 2000, see page 211.

Using Wizards

You can also use another approach. Click Programs in step 1. In step 2, select a program. Now follow steps 3-4.

Works Suite 2000 provides a large number of Wizards, organised under overall category headings. With these, you can create a wide variety of professional-quality documents (Works Suite 2000 calls this carrying out tasks). For example, you can create recipe books, home inventories, fax cover sheets, brochures, flyers, menus, newsletters, school reports, invitations, student schedules, errand lists, graph paper, financial worksheets . . .

For how to run the Task Launcher in non-principal modules, see page 15.

Basing new documents on a Wizard

In any principal Works Suite 2000 module (except Calendar), pull down the File menu and click New. The Task Launcher appears. Carry out the following steps:

You can also launch specific Internet-related tasks. For example, you can:

• set up a new Internet connection

• read your Outlook Express email

• play online games, and;

• view online news

In step 1, select Programs. In step 2, select MSN, Internet Explorer or Outlook Express. In step 3, choose a Web task. Finally, carry out step 4 and follow the on-screen instructions.

1 Select Tasks

3 Select a task

2 Select a task heading

4 Click Start

The section on the right of the Task Launcher provides a potted description of the selected task.

You can use a wizard approach in Home Publishing 2000.

In the Home Publishing Home screen (if you aren't here, press Ctrl+N), click the appropriate tab on the left – e.g. to create a Web project, click this tab:

On the right of the screen, click a task button – e.g. to create Web pages, click:

In the Themes box, select a theme (e.g. Just for Fun). On the right of the screen, select a template and click OK. Home Publishing opens the template in a new window; make the relevant amendments. (For how to do this, see chapter 6.)

To use a wizard approach in Picture It! Express, click the Projects tab. In the tab, select a heading (e.g. Fun Stuff). In the fly-out, click a project type. In the next screen, select a specific project and click Next. Now follow the on-screen instructions to edit your new picture.

When you've selected the Wizard you want to use, Works Suite 2000 launches a dialog which varies accordingly. However, the basic format is the same. Works is asking you to supply it with the information required by making the relevant choices.

Carry out the following steps:

5 Make the relevant choice

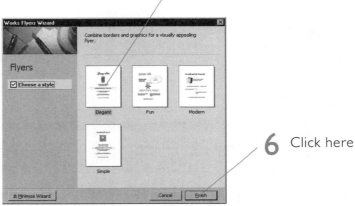

6 Click here

The end result:

Here, a flyer has been created in Word 2000

Creating your own templates

In any of the principal Works Suite 2000 modules (apart from the Calendar), you can save an existing document (complete with all text and formatting) as a template. You can then use this template as the basis for new document creation. The text/formatting is immediately carried across.

To save your work as a template in Word, follow step 1. Instead of following steps 2-4, however, click in the Save as type: field and select Document Template (*.dot). In the File name: field, name the new template.
Finally, click Save.

Saving your work as a template

First, open the document you want to save as a template (for how to do this, see the 'Opening Works Suite 2000 documents' topic later). Pull down the File menu and click Save As. Now do the following:

| Click here. In the drop-down list, click the drive you want to host the template

To use a template you've created, follow the procedures on page 20.

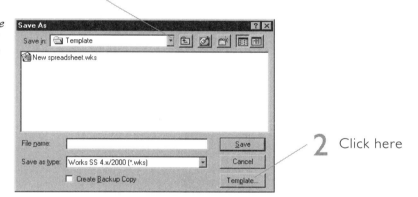

2 Click here

Re step 2 – you may have to double-click one or more folders first, to locate the folder you want to host the new template.

4 Click here

3 Name the new template

Using your templates

Any templates you create are automatically accessible from the Task Launcher under the heading 'Personal Templates'.

Opening a template

In the Task Launcher (either when you've just started Works Suite 2000 or after you've started the Launcher manually), carry out the following steps:

| Select Tasks   3 Select a template

2 Select Personal   4 Click Start
Templates

Opening Works Suite 2000 documents

You can also use the Documents section of the Windows Startup menu to open recently used Works files – see your Windows documentation for how to do this.

We saw earlier that Works Suite 2000 lets you create new documents in various ways. You can also open Word, Spreadsheet and Database documents you've already created:

- just after you've started Works Suite 2000

- from within the relevant Works Suite 2000 module

Opening an existing document at startup

Immediately after you've started Works, carry out steps 1 and 2:

Although you can create and save files in Picture It! Express, and routes in AutoRoute Express, they do not appear in the History section of the Task Launcher.

(For more on opening routes in AutoRoute Express, see page 222.)

To view entries in a different order, click a column heading. Now do the following:

Date ▲

Click here to switch from Ascending to Descending view (or vice versa)

As an example, to sort items alphabetically by program module, click the Program heading. Then click the arrow to select Ascending or Descending as the sort order.

1 Click History

Column headings

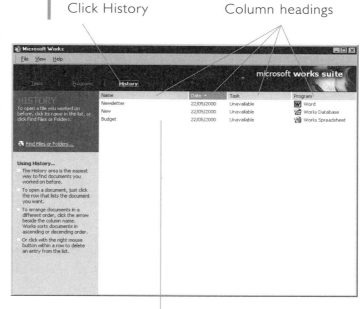

2 Click the row which represents the file you want to open

To open files in Picture It! Express, Home Publishing or Money, press Ctrl+O. Use the resulting dialog to locate and open the relevant file.

(See page 222 for how to open routes in AutoRoute Express.)

The Open dialog is rather different in Word.

Re step 3 – you may have to double-click one or more folders first, to locate the file you want to open.

You can open ('import') documents created in formats native to other programs into any Works Suite 2000 module (except AutoRoute Express and Encarta World Atlas). For example, you can import HTML or Works 2000 Word Processor files...

In step 1, select the external format. Then follow steps 2-3.

(In the case of Calendar, however, use a slightly different route. Click Import in the File menu and then follow steps 2-3.

Opening a document from within a module

From within any principal Works Suite 2000 module except Calendar, pull down the File menu and click Open. Now carry out the following steps, as appropriate:

2 Click here. In the drop-down list, click the drive which hosts the file

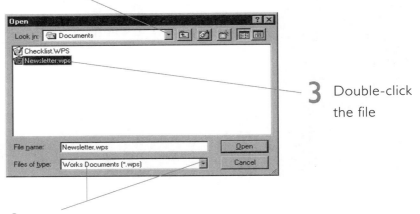

3 Double-click the file

Make sure the appropriate entry – e.g. All Files (*.*) in Word – is shown here. If it isn't, click the arrow and select it in the list

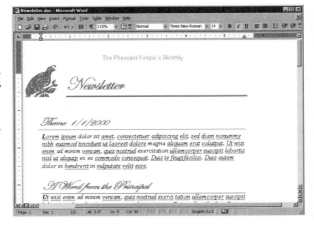

The opened newsletter

Saving Works Suite 2000 documents

You can save Works Suite 2000 documents in formats which can be utilised by other programs (this is called 'exporting'). For example, you can save files into HTML format, for use on the World Wide Web.

After step 1, click in the Save as type: field. In the drop-down list, select the external format. Then follow steps 2-3.

For how to save routes in AutoRoute Express 2000, see page 222.

Re step 2 – you may have to double-click one or more folders first, to locate the folder you want to host the new file.

To perform initial saves in Picture It! Express, press Ctrl+S. In Section 1 of the Save As dialog, select a destination folder. In 2, select an output format. In 3, name the file. In 4, type in optional descriptive text. Finally, click:

Save

It's important to save your work at frequent intervals, in order to avoid data loss in the event of a hardware fault or power interruption. With the exception of the Calendar and Money (which save work automatically) and Encarta World Atlas, Works Suite 2000 uses a broadly consistent approach to saving throughout its modules.

Saving a document for the first time

In any of the principal modules apart from Calendar (or in Home Publishing 2000), pull down the File menu and click Save. Or press Ctrl+S. Now do the following:

1 Click here. In the drop-down list, click the drive you want to host the file

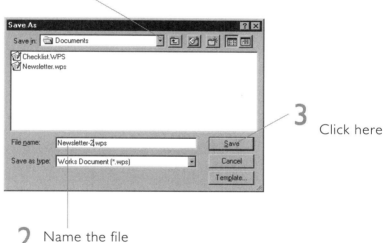

3 Click here

2 Name the file

Saving previously saved documents

In any of the principal modules apart from Calendar (or in Home Publishing 2000 or AutoRoute Express) pull down the File menu and click Save. Or press Ctrl+S. No dialog launches; instead, Works Suite 2000 saves the latest version of your document to disk, overwriting the previous version.

Sending documents via email

To send a Home Publishing file as an e-mail attachment, use a different procedure.
Pull down the File menu and click Send by E-mail. In the Send By Email dialog, double-click As an attachment in an e-mail message. Follow the on-screen instructions.

You can send almost any Works Suite 2000 file as an email attachment. When you do this, Works launches a new message in your email program – the Works document is automatically attached.

Emailing a Works Suite 2000 file

Within any principal Works module, pull down the File menu and do the following:

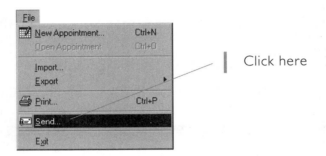

Click here

Re step 1 – in Word, select Send To, Mail Recipient (As Attachment) instead.

2 Complete any dialog which launches (in Calendar, select a style and date range), then click OK

Re step 2 – in Picture It! Express, follow step 1. Select Put the picture in an e-mail message in the dialog, then click Done. Finally, follow steps 3-4.

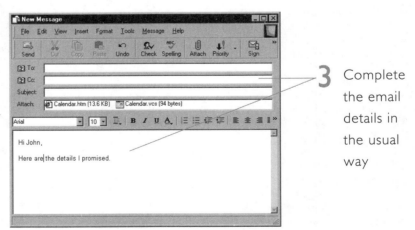

Here, Outlook Express is being used to send a Works Suite 2000 calendar as an attachment.

3 Complete the email details in the usual way

4 Complete any further options as necessary, then click Send

Word 2000

This chapter gives you the basics of using Word 2000. You'll learn how to enter text, send e-mail and work with the Word screen. You'll also format text and use text styles. Finally, you'll proof your documents, create summaries, bookmarks and hyperlinks, insert pictures, customise page layout and printing and use the Office Assistant.

Covers

Chapter Two

The Word 2000 screen

Below is a detailed illustration of the Word 2000 screen.

Title bar   Menu bar

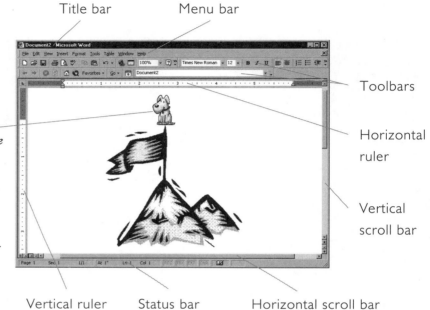

Toolbars

Horizontal ruler

Vertical scroll bar

This is an incarnation of the Word Assistant – see pages 94-96.

The Status bar displays information relating to the active document (e.g. what page you're on).

Vertical ruler   Status bar   Horizontal scroll bar

Some of these – e.g. the rulers and scroll bars – are standard to just about all programs that run under Windows. Many of them can be hidden, if required.

Specifying which screen components display

Pull down the Tools menu and click Options. Then:

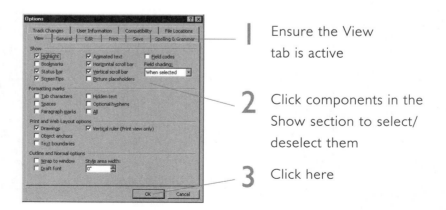

1 Ensure the View tab is active

2 Click components in the Show section to select/ deselect them

3 Click here

Entering text

You can also use Click and Type to enter text almost anywhere in a document, without inserting the necessary paragraph marks or formatting – see pages 28-29.

Word 2000 lets you enter text immediately after you've started it (you can do this because a new blank document is automatically created based on the default template). In Word, you enter text at the insertion point:

A magnified view of the Word text insertion point

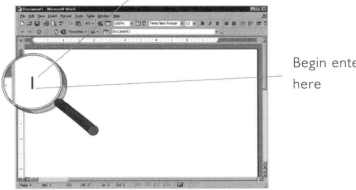

Begin entering text here

You can have Word 2000 insert words/phrases for you. Place the insertion point where you want the text inserted. Pull down the Insert menu and click AutoText. In the sub-menu, click a category (e.g. Salutation) then a glossary entry (e.g. Dear Sir or Madam); Word inserts the entry.

Additional characters

Most of the text you need to enter can be typed in directly from the keyboard. However, it's sometimes necessary to enter special characters, e.g. bullets (for instance: ✐) or special symbols like ©.

Pull down the Insert menu and click Symbol. Now do the following:

1 Ensure the Symbols tab is active

2 Click here; select the appropriate font from the list

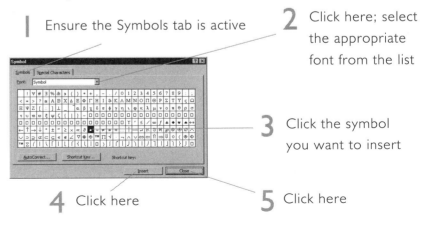

3 Click the symbol you want to insert

4 Click here

5 Click here

Click and Type

You can also enter text in a special way in Word 2000, one that makes the process much easier. With Click and Type:

- you can enter text or pictures in most blank page areas, with the minimum of mouse activity

- you don't have to apply the necessary formatting yourself – Word 2000 does this automatically (e.g. you can insert text to the right of an existing paragraph without having to insert manual tab stops)

Using Click and Type

Ensure you're using Web Layout or Print Layout view. Position the mouse pointer where you want to insert text or a picture. Click once – the pointer changes to indicate the formatting which Word 2000 will apply:

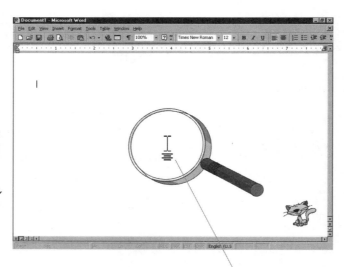

Here, the pointer shows that Word 2000 is about to centre new text...

Now double-click, then do the following:

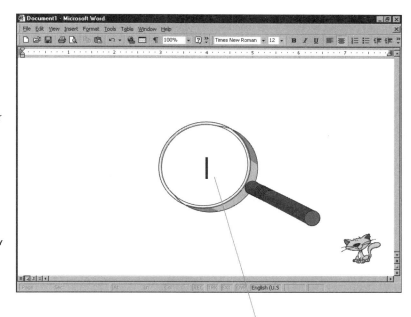

If you use Click and Type beneath an existing text paragraph, Word 2000 applies a specific style to the new text. You can specify the style used.

Pull down the Tools menu and click Options. In the Options dialog, activate the Edit tab. In the Click and type section, click in this field:

In the drop-down list, select a style. Finally, click OK.

Begin entering text, or insert a picture in the normal way

The Click and Type pointers

The main pointers are:

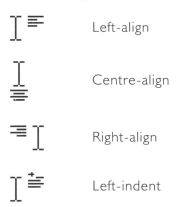

Left-align

Centre-align

Right-align

Left-indent

Sending e-mail

You can use Word to write and send e-mail messages (provided you also have Microsoft Outlook 2000 installed).

Pull down the File menu and click Send To, Mail Recipient. Now do the following:

I Type in the recipient's e-mail address

2 Type in a subject

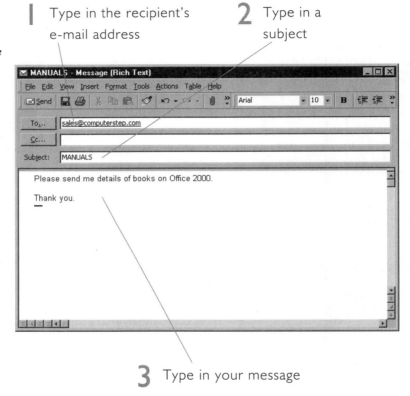

3 Type in your message

4 Click this toolbar button: ☰ Send

Moving around in documents

You can use the following to move through Word 2000 documents:

- keystrokes

- the vertical/horizontal scroll bars

- the Go To section of the Find and Replace dialog

The keystroke route

Word implements the standard Windows direction keys. Use the left, right, up and down cursor keys in the usual way. Additionally, Home, End, Page Up and Page Down work normally.

The scroll bar route

Use your mouse to perform any of the following actions:

To move to the location where you last made an amendment, press Shift+F5. You can do this as many as three times in succession.

When you drag the box on the vertical scroll bar, Word displays a page indicator (magnified in the illustration) showing which page you're up to.

Click anywhere here to jump to another location in the document

Click anywhere here to jump to another location in the document

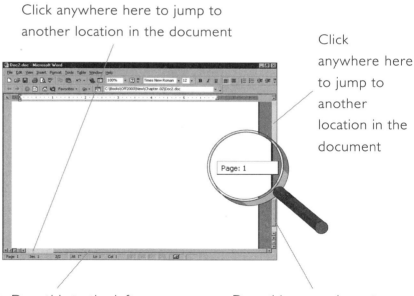

Drag this to the left or right to extend the viewing area

Drag this up or down to move through the active document

The dialog route

You can use the Go To tab in the Find and Replace dialog to move to a variety of document locations. These include:

- pages (probably the most common)

- lines

- pictures

You can use a keyboard shortcut to launch the Go To dialog: simply press Ctrl+G.

Pull down the Edit menu and click Go To. Now do the following:

| Click the location type you want to go to   **3** Click here

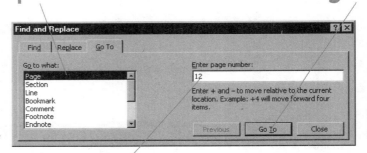

To have Word count the words in the active document, pull down the Tools menu and click Word Count. This is the result:

Click here to close

2 Type in the specific location reference (e.g. a number if you selected 'Page' in step 1)

There are some useful refinements:

- You can enter *relative* movements in step 2. For example, if you want to move seventeen pages back from the present location, type in -17. Or +5 to move five pages forward…

- To move to the next or previous instance of the specified location (i.e. without specifying a reference), omit step 2. In step 3, the dialog is now slightly different; click Next or Previous, as appropriate. Click Close when you've finished.

Views

Word 2000 also provides another view which you'll use frequently: Print Preview.
See pages 85-88 for more information.

Word 2000 lets you examine your work in various ways, according to the approach you need. It calls these 'views'. The principal views are:

Normal

Normal View – the default – is used for basic text editing. In Normal View, text formatting elements are still visible; for instance, coloured, emboldened or italicised text displays faithfully. However, little attempt is made to show document structure or layout (for example, headers/footers and pictures are invisible). For these reasons, Normal View is quick and easy to use. It's suitable for bulk text entry and editing. Not recommended for use with graphics.

Print Layout

Print Layout view works like Normal view, with one exception: the positioning of items on the page is reproduced accurately. Headers/footers and pictures are visible, and can be edited directly; margins display faithfully.

In Print Layout view, the screen is updated more slowly. Use it when your document is nearing completion.

Web Layout

In Web layout view, Web pages are optimised so that they appear as they will when published to the Web or an Intranet. Effects which are often used on the Web display e.g. backgrounds and AutoShapes.

The stationery shown in the illustration can be found in the following folder:
Program Files\Common Files\Microsoft Shared\ Stationery
(When viewed in Normal or Print Layout views, this file displays much less detail.)

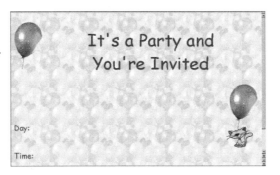

Word 2000 displaying a stationery (HTML) file

When Full Screen view is active, you lose access to toolbars and scroll bars. However, you can still access the menus by using the keyboard (e.g. Alt+F to launch the File menu).

Full Screen

Unless you have a particularly large monitor, you'll probably find that there are times when your screen is too cluttered. Full Screen view hides all standard screen components in one operation, thereby making more space available for editing.

Use Full Screen view when you need it, as an adjunct to Normal or Print Layout view.

Summarising documents

In effect, Word provides another way to view a document: you can 'summarise' it. When you summarise a document, Word 2000:

Summarising – as part of Word 2000's Install on Demand feature –may not be installed. If it isn't, Word launches a special message (if the Assistant is on-screen – if not, a standard message appears):

- analyses it and allocates a 'score' to each sentence
- allocates a higher score for sentences which contain repeated words

After this, you specify what percentage of the higher-scoring sentences you want to display.

To summarise the active document, pull down the Tools menu and click AutoSummarize. Word 2000 carries out the initial analysis. When it's completed, do the following:

Click Yes and follow the on-screen instructions. Then carry out steps 1-3.

(See page 80 for more on Install on Demand; see pages 94-96 for how to use the Assistant).

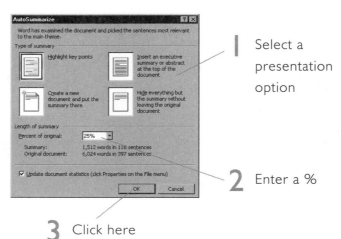

Select a presentation option

2 Enter a %

3 Click here

Implementing views

Switching to Normal, Web Layout or Print Layout views

Pull down the View menu and do the following:

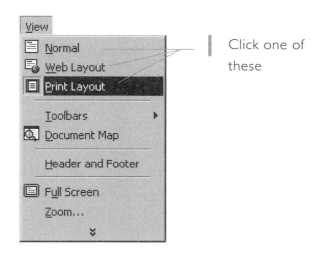

Click one of these

Switching to Full Screen view

Pull down the View menu and do the following:

To leave Full Screen view, press Esc or do the following in the on-screen toolbar:

Click here

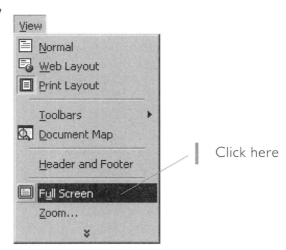

Click here

Changing zoom levels

The ability to vary the level of magnification for the active document is often useful. Sometimes, it's helpful to 'zoom out' (i.e. decrease the magnification) so that you can take an overview; at other times, you'll need to 'zoom in' (increase the magnification) to work in greater detail. Word 2000 lets you do either of these very easily.

You can do any of the following:

- choose from preset zoom levels (e.g. 100%, 75%)

- specify your own zoom percentage

- choose Many Pages, to view a specific number of pages

Setting the zoom level

Pull down the View menu and click Zoom. Now carry out steps 1 or 2 (to specify a zoom %) OR 3 & 4 (to specify a group of pages). Finally, in either case, follow step 5.

The Preview section on the right provides an indication of what the selected view level looks like.

Click a preset zoom level

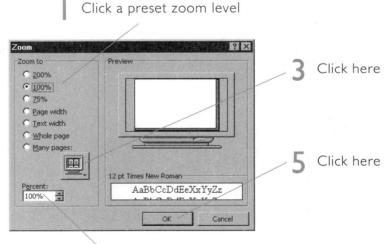

3 Click here

5 Click here

Re step 2 – entries here must lie in the range: 10%-500%

2 Type in your own zoom percentage

4 Click a multiple-page view

Formatting text – an overview

Word 2000 lets you format text in a variety of ways. Broadly, however, text formatting can be divided into two overall categories:

You can have Word 2000 format the active document automatically.

Pull down the Tools menu and click AutoCorrect. In the AutoCorrect dialog, click the AutoFormat tab. Specify the type(s) of formatting you want applied. Finally, click OK.

Character formatting

Character formatting is concerned with altering the *appearance* of selected text. Examples include:

- changing the font and type size

- colouring text

- changing the font style (bold, italic etc.)

- underlining text

- applying font effects (superscript, subscript, small caps etc.)

Character formatting is a misnomer in one sense: it can also be applied to specific paragraphs of text.

Paragraph formatting

Paragraph formatting has to do with the structuring and layout of paragraphs of text. Examples include:

Whenever you type in Internet paths – e.g.: http://www. ineasysteps.com (without the break) – AutoFormat automatically implements them as hypertext links. This means that clicking an address takes you there (if your Internet link is currently open).

- specifying paragraph indents

- specifying paragraph alignment (e.g. left or right justification)

- specifying paragraph and line spacing

- imposing borders and/or fills on paragraphs

The term "paragraph formatting" is also something of a misnomer in that some of these – for instance, line-spacing – can also be applied to the whole of the active document rather than selected paragraphs.

Changing the font or type size

Character formatting can be changed in two ways:

- from within the Font dialog

- (to a lesser extent) by using the Formatting toolbar

Word 2000 uses standard Windows procedures for text selection.

Applying a new font/type size – the dialog route

First, select the text whose typeface and/or type size you want to amend. Pull down the Format menu and click Font. Now carry out step 1. Perform step 2 and/or 3. Finally, carry out step 4:

| Ensure the Font tab is active

Re step 3 – as well as whole point sizes, you can also enter half-point increments. For instance, Word 2000 will accept:

10, 10.5 or 11

but not:

10.7 or 10.85.

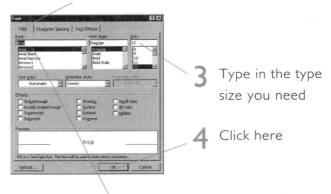

3 Type in the type size you need

4 Click here

2 Click the font you want to use

If the Formatting toolbar isn't currently visible, pull down the View menu and click Toolbars, Formatting.

Applying a new font/type size – the toolbar route

Make sure the Formatting toolbar is visible. Now select the text you want to amend and do the following:

Click here; select the font you want to use in the drop-down list

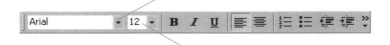

Type in the type size you need and press Enter

Changing text colour

First, select the text you want to alter. Pull down the Format menu and click Font. Now do the following:

1 Ensure the Font tab is active

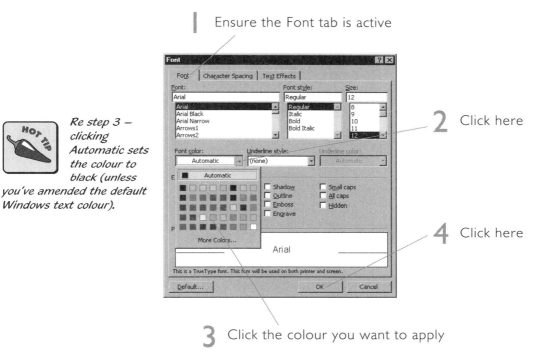

Re step 3 – clicking Automatic sets the colour to black (unless you've amended the default Windows text colour).

2 Click here

4 Click here

3 Click the colour you want to apply

Verifying current text formatting

If you're in any doubt about what character/paragraph formatting attributes are associated with text, press Shift+F1. Now click in the text. This is the result:

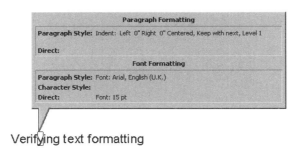

Verifying text formatting

Press Esc to return to normal text editing.

Changing the font style

The default font style is Regular. The additional font styles you can use depend on the typeface. For example, Times New Roman has Bold, Italic and Bold Italic. Arial Rounded MT Bold, on the other hand, just has Bold and Bold Italic.

You can use the Font dialog or the Formatting toolbar to change font styles.

Amending the font style – the dialog route

First, select the text whose style you want to change. Then pull down the Format menu and click Font. Do the following:

To underline text, click here. Select an underlining type in the list.

The Preview section provides an indication of what the amendments you make look like.

Ensure the Font tab is active

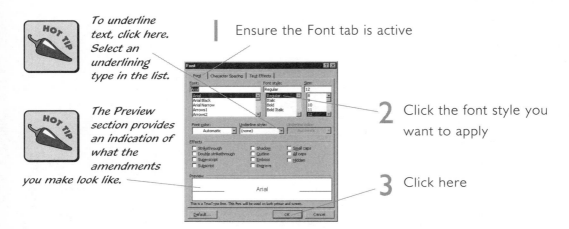

2 Click the font style you want to apply

3 Click here

Amending the font style – the toolbar route

First, select the relevant text. Ensure the Formatting toolbar is visible. Then do any of the following:

If the Formatting toolbar isn't visible, pull down the View menu and click Toolbars, Formatting.

Click here to embolden the text

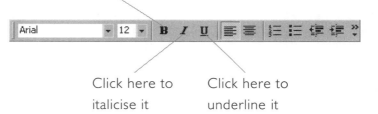

Click here to italicise it

Click here to underline it

Font effects

The following are the principal font effects:

- Strikethrough – e.g. ~~font effect~~

- Superscript – e.g. f$^{\text{ont effect}}$

- Subscript – e.g. f$_{\text{ont effect}}$

- All Caps – e.g. FONT EFFECT

- Small Caps – e.g. FONT EFFECT

In addition, you can mark text as hidden, which means that it doesn't display on screen or print.

Applying font effects

First, select the relevant text. Pull down the Format menu and click Font. Then carry out the following steps:

You can also use the following keyboard shortcuts:

Ctrl++	Superscript
Ctrl+=	Subscript
Ctrl+Shift +K	Small Caps
Ctrl+Shift +A	All Caps
Ctrl+Shift +H	Hidden

Many of the font effects can be combined – e.g. Superscript with Small Caps. However, Small Caps and All Caps are mutually exclusive.

Ensure the Font tab is active

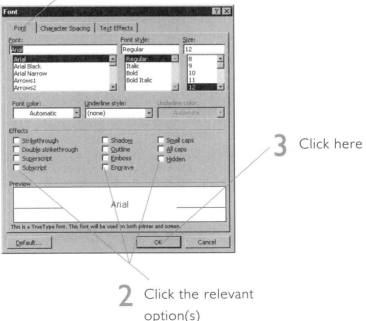

3 Click here

2 Click the relevant option(s)

Indenting paragraphs – an overview

Indents are a crucial component of document layout. For instance, in most document types indenting the first line of paragraphs (i.e. moving it inwards away from the left page margin) makes the text much more legible.

You can achieve a similar effect by using tabs. However, indents are easier to apply (and amend subsequently).

Other document types – e.g. bibliographies – can use the following:

- negative indents (where the direction of indent is towards and beyond the left margin)

- hanging indents (where the first line is unaltered, while subsequent lines are indented)

- full indents (where the entire paragraph is indented away from the left and/or the right margins)

Don't confuse indents with page margins. Margins are the gap between the edge of the page and the text area; indents define the distance between the margins and text.

Some of the potential indent combinations are shown in the illustration below:

> **This paragraph has a full left and right indent. It's best, however, not to overdo the extent of the indent: 0.35 inches is often more than adequate.**
>
> **This paragraph has a first-line indent. This type of indent is suitable for most document types. It's best, however, not to overdo the extent of the indent: 0.35 inches is often more than adequate.**
>
> **This paragraph has a negative left indent. It's best, however, not to overdo the extent of the indent: 0.35 inches is often more than adequate.**
>
> **This paragraph has a hanging indent. It's best, however, not to overdo the extent of the indent: 0.35 inches is often more than adequate.**

left and right indent

first-line indent

negative left indent

hanging indent

Left margin (inserted for illustration purposes)

Right margin (inserted for illustration purposes)

Applying indents to paragraphs

Paragraphs can be indented from within the Paragraph dialog or (to an extent) by using the Formatting toolbar.

Indenting text – the dialog route

First, select the paragraph(s) you want to indent. Pull down the Format menu and click Paragraph. Now follow step 1 below. If you want a left indent, carry out step 2. For a right indent, follow step 3. To achieve a first-line or hanging indent, follow steps 4 and 5. Finally, irrespective of the indent type, carry out step 6.

Ensure this tab is active

Re steps 2 and 3 – type in minus values for negative indents.

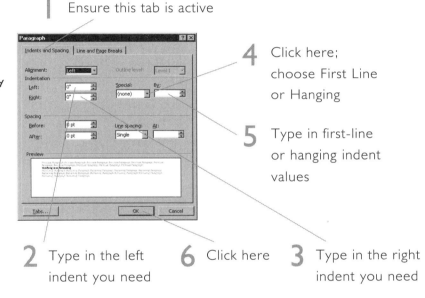

4 Click here; choose First Line or Hanging

5 Type in first-line or hanging indent values

2 Type in the left indent you need

6 Click here

3 Type in the right indent you need

If the Formatting toolbar isn't visible, pull down the View menu and click Toolbars, Formatting.

Indenting text – the toolbar route

First, select the relevant paragraph(s). Ensure the Formatting toolbar is visible. Then click one of these:

Indents the paragraph(s) to the next tab stop

Indents the paragraph(s) to the previous tab stop

Aligning paragraphs

You can adjust alignment from within the Paragraph dialog, or by the use of the Formatting toolbar.

Word 2000 supports the following types of alignment:

Left alignment
Text is flush with the left page margin.

Right alignment
Text is flush with the right page margin.

Justification
Text is flush with the left *and* right page margins.

Centred
Text is placed evenly between the left/right page margins.

Aligning text – the dialog route
First, select the paragraph(s) you want to align. Pull down the Format menu and click Paragraph. Now:

Re the HOT TIP below – if you've used the Right Align or Justify buttons before, Word 2000 may have promoted them to the main body of the Formatting toolbar.

Ensure the Indents and Spacing tab is active

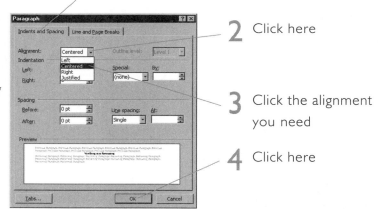

2 Click here

3 Click the alignment you need

4 Click here

To right-align or justify the selected text, click ⁑ on the right of the toolbar. In the flyout, click one of these:

Right align

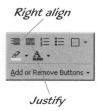

Justify

Aligning text – the toolbar route
Select the relevant paragraph(s). Then click one of these:

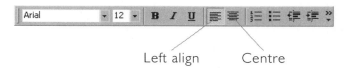

Left align   Centre

Specifying paragraph spacing

As a general rule, set low paragraph spacing settings: a little goes a long way.

Word 2000 lets you customise the vertical space before and/ or after specific text paragraphs. This is a useful device for increasing text legibility.

By default, Word defines paragraph spacing – like type sizes – in point sizes. However, if you want you can enter measurements in different units. To do this, apply any of the following suffixes to values you enter:

- in – for inches e.g. '2 in'
- cm – for centimetres e.g. '5 cm'
- pi – for picas e.g. '14 pi'
- px – for pixels e.g. '50 px' (about ½ inch)

Note that the following definitions should be useful:

- Picas are an alternative measure in typography: one pica is almost equivalent to one-sixth inch. Picas are often used to define line length, and;

- Pixels (a contraction of 'picture elements') are the smallest components of the picture on a computer monitor

Applying paragraph spacing

First, select the paragraph you want to space. Pull down the Format menu and click Paragraph. Now carry out the steps below:

1 Ensure the Indents and Spacing tab is active

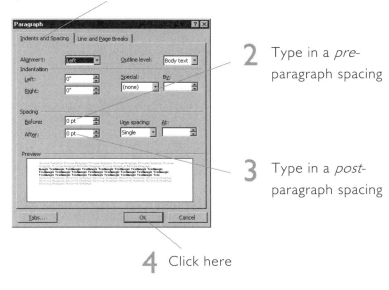

2 Type in a *pre-*paragraph spacing

3 Type in a *post-*paragraph spacing

4 Click here

Line spacing – an overview

Line spacing is also known as leading (pronounced 'ledding').

It's often necessary to amend line spacing. This is the vertical distance between individual lines of text, or more accurately between the baseline (the imaginary line on which text appears to sit) of one line and the baseline of the previous.

Word 2000 lets you apply a variety of line spacing settings:

Single

Word 2000 separates each line of type by an amount which is slightly more than the type size. For example, if the text is in 12 points, the gap between lines is just over 12 points. Newspapers, particularly, use single line spacing.

This is Word 2000's default.

1.5 Lines

150% of single line spacing.

Double

200% of single line spacing. Manuscripts of all descriptions are nearly always prepared with double line spacing.

At Least

Sets the minimum line height at the value you specify; Word 2000 can adjust the line spacing to fit the constituent character sizes.

Exactly

Sets the value you specify as an unvarying line height: Word 2000 cannot adjust it.

Multiple

Sets line height as a multiple of single-spaced text. For example, specifying "3.5" here initiates a line height of 3.5 lines.

Adjusting line spacing

First, select the relevant paragraph(s). Then move the mouse pointer over them and right-click. Do the following:

If you've just created a new document, you can set the line spacing before you begin to enter text. With the insertion point at the start of the document, follow the procedures outlined here.

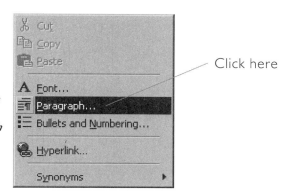

Click here

Now perform step 1 below. If you want to apply a preset spacing, follow step 2. To implement your own spacing, carry out steps 3 and 4 instead. Finally, follow step 5:

1 Ensure the Indents and Spacing tab is active

You can use these keyboard shortcuts to adjust line spacing:

Ctrl+1   *Single spacing*

Ctrl+5   *1 ½ spacing*

Ctrl+2   *Double spacing*

2 Click here; choose Single, 1.5 Lines or Double in the list

4 If you followed step 3, type in the amount of line spacing

3 Click here; choose At Least, Exactly or Multiple in the list

5 Click here

Paragraph borders

By default, Word 2000 does not border paragraph text. However, you can apply a wide selection of borders if you want. You can specify:

- the type and thickness of the border

- how many sides the border should have

- the border colour

- whether the text is shadowed or in 3-D

- the distance of the border from the text

Applying a border

First, select the paragraph(s) you want to border. Then pull down the Format menu and click Borders and Shading. Carry out step 1 below. Now carry out steps 2-5, as appropriate. Finally, perform step 6:

You can also border selected text within a paragraph. However, the Borders tab is then slightly different (e.g. you can't deselect the border for specific sides).

To set the distance from the border to the enclosed text, click Options. Insert the relevant distances and click OK. Then follow step 6.

Use step 5 to deselect the top, bottom, left or right paragraph borders. If you want to deselect more than one, repeat step 5 as often as necessary.

1 Ensure the Borders tab is active

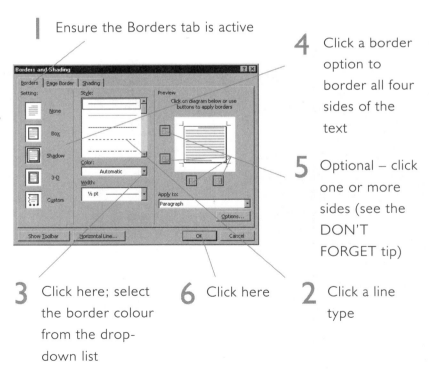

4 Click a border option to border all four sides of the text

5 Optional – click one or more sides (see the DON'T FORGET tip)

3 Click here; select the border colour from the drop-down list

6 Click here

2 Click a line type

Paragraph fills

By default, Word 2000 does not apply a fill to text paragraphs. However, you can do the following if you want:

- specify a percentage fill e.g. 20% (light grey) or 85% (very dark grey)

- apply a simple pattern, if required

- specify a background fill colour

- specify a pattern colour

Applying a fill

First, select the paragraph(s) you want to fill. Then pull down the Format menu and click Borders and Shading. Now carry out step 1 below. Follow steps 2, 3 or 4 as appropriate. Finally, carry out step 5:

1 Ensure the Shading tab is active

4 Click a background fill colour

Re steps 3 and 4 – you can achieve unique blends by applying different pattern and background colours.

2 Click here; select a % fill or pattern from the list

3 Click here; select a pattern colour from the drop-down list

5 Click here

Working with tabs

Tabs are a means of indenting the first line of text paragraphs (you can also use indents for this purpose – see pages 42-43).

When you press the Tab key while the text-insertion point is at the start of a paragraph, the text in the first line jumps to the next tab stop – see the illustration below:

Never use the Space Bar to indent paragraphs: spaces vary in size according to the typeface and type size applying to specific paragraphs, and therefore give uneven results.

Never use the Space Bar to indent paragraphs: spaces vary in size according to the typeface and type size applying to specific paragraphs, and therefore give uneven results.

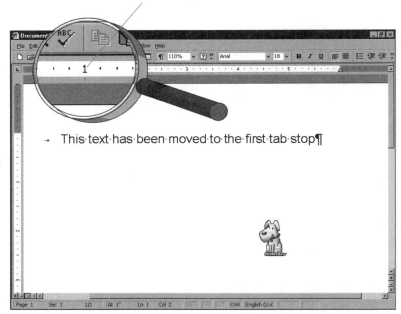

The first tab stop

This text has been moved to the first tab stop¶

You should note that the inserted tab is denoted by this symbol on the left of the text:

To have tab stops (and other symbols) display, pull down the Tools menu and click Options. Activate the View tab, then select All in the Formatting marks section. Finally, click OK.

Inserting tabs is a useful way to increase the legibility of your text. Word 2000 lets you set tab stops with great precision.

By default, Word 2000 inserts tab stops automatically every half an inch. If you want, you can enter new or revised tab stop positions individually.

Setting tab stops

First, select the paragraph(s) in which you need to set tab stops. Pull down the Format menu and click Tabs. Now carry out step 1 below. If you want to implement a new default tab stop position, follow step 2. If, on the other hand, you need to set up individual tab stops, carry out steps 3 AND 4 as often as necessary. Finally, in either case, follow step 5 to confirm your changes.

When you've performed steps 3 and 4, the individual tab stop position appears here:

2 Type in the new tab stop default (e.g. 0.35")

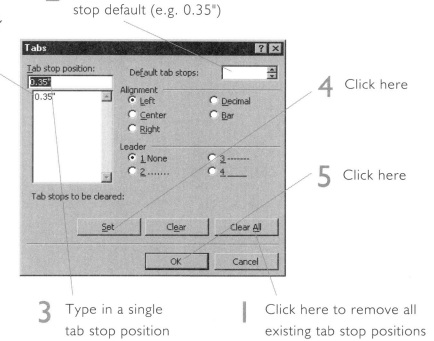

4 Click here

5 Click here

3 Type in a single tab stop position

| Click here to remove all existing tab stop positions

Searching for text

Word 2000 lets you search for specific text within the active document. Even better, however, you can also search for character or paragraph formatting, either separately from the text search or at the same time.

For example, you can if you want have Word locate all instances of the word 'information'. Or you could have it find all italicised words, whatever they are. Similarly, you could have it flag all instances of '*information*'.

You can also:

- limit the search to words which match the case of the text you specify (e.g. if you search for 'Man', Word will not flag 'man' or 'MAN')

- limit the search to whole words (e.g. if you search for 'nation', Word will not flag 'international')

- have Word search for word forms (e.g. if you look for 'began', Word will also stop at 'begin', 'begun' and 'beginning')

- have Word search for homophones (e.g. if you look for 'there', Word will flag 'their')

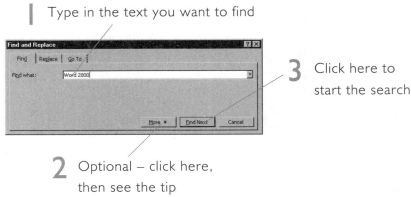

Follow step 2 to locate specific formatting. In the extended dialog which launches, click Format. Word 2000 launches a menu; click the relevant entry. Then complete the dialog which appears in the normal way. Finally, follow step 3 to begin the search.

Initiating a text search

Pull down the Edit menu and click Find. Now do the following:

1 Type in the text you want to find

3 Click here to start the search

2 Optional – click here, then see the tip

Replacing text

When you've located text and/or formatting, you can have Word 2000 replace it automatically with the text and/or formatting of your choice.

You can customise find-and-replace operations with the same parameters as a simple Find operation. For example, you can have Word find every occurrence of 'information' and replace it with '*information*', or even '*data*'...

Initiating a find-and-replace operation

First pull down the Edit menu and click Replace. In the Find and Replace dialog, click More. Now follow steps 1 and 2 below. Carry out steps 3 and/or 4, as appropriate. Finally, follow either step 5 OR 6:

1 Type in the text you want to find

2 Type in the replacement text

5 Click here to replace the first instance of the specified text

This is the extended version of the dialog which may not appear by default. To make it appear, click this button:

More ∓

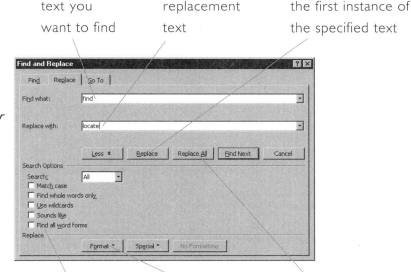

When you follow step 3, Word launches a menu; click the relevant entry. Then complete the dialog which appears in the normal way. Finally, carry out step 5 OR 6, as appropriate.

4 Specify the parameters you need

3 Click here to replace formatting

6 Or click here to replace all instances of the specified text

Working with headers

You can have Word 2000 print text at the top of each page within a document; this area is called the 'header'. In the same way, you can have text printed at the base of each page (the 'footer'). Headers and footers are printed within the top and bottom page margins, respectively.

To edit an existing header, simply follow the procedures outlined on the right; in step 1, amend the current header text as necessary.

When you create a header, Word automatically switches the active document to Print Layout view and displays the Header and Footer toolbar.

Inserting a header

Move to the start of your document. Pull down the View menu and click Header and Footer. Do any of the following:

Header text can be formatted in the normal way. For instance, you can apply a new font and/or type size...

You can have Word 2000 insert a special code which automatically inserts the page number in the header – see step 2.

1 Type in the Header text

4 Click here to return to normal document editing

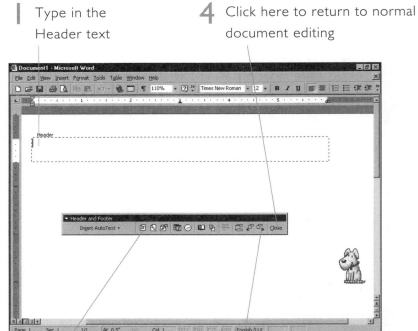

2 Click here to insert a page number code

3 Optional – click here to move to the header on the next page

Working with footers

When you create a footer, Word 2000 automatically switches the active document to Print Layout view and displays the Header and Footer toolbar.

Inserting a footer

Move to the start of your document. Pull down the View menu and click Header and Footer. Word launches the Header and Footer toolbar over the footer area. To create a footer, do the following:

Click here

Word 2000 moves to the footer area. Do any of the following:

2 Click here to insert a page number code

3 Optional – click here to move to the footer on the next page

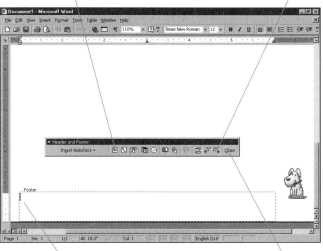

1 Type in the footer text

4 Click here to return to normal document editing

Inserting bookmarks

In computer terms, a bookmark is a marker inserted to enable you to find a given location in a document easily and quickly.

Creating a bookmark

Place the insertion point where you want the bookmark inserted. Pull down the Insert menu and click Bookmark. Now do the following:

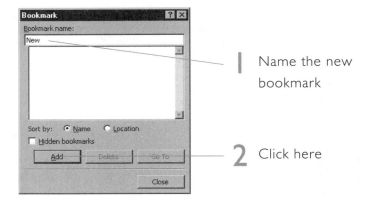

1 Name the new bookmark

2 Click here

Jumping to a bookmark

Pull down the Insert menu and click Bookmark. Now do the following:

To delete a bookmark, carry out step 1 on the immediate right. Click this button:

Then follow step 3.

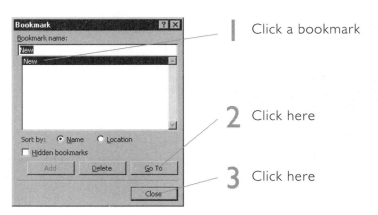

1 Click a bookmark

2 Click here

3 Click here

Inserting hyperlinks

You can insert hyperlinks into Word documents. Hyperlinks are text or graphics linked to:

- another location (e.g. a pre-inserted bookmark) in the same document, or;

- a document on the World Wide Web or an Intranet

Creating a hyperlink to a bookmark

Select the text or graphic you want to be the source of the link. Pull down the Insert menu and do the following:

To amend a bookmark hyperlink, place the insertion point within it (for text hyperlinks) or select the picture (for picture hyperlinks). Follow steps 1-2. In step 3, make the necessary changes. Finally, carry out step 4.

To delete a bookmark hyperlink, place the insertion point within it (for text hyperlinks) or select the picture (for picture hyperlinks). Follow steps 1-2. Now click this button:

1 Click here

2 Click Place in This Document

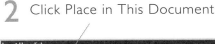

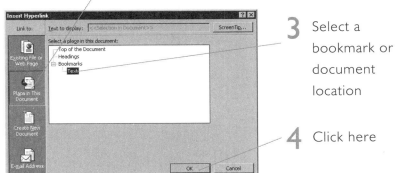

3 Select a bookmark or document location

4 Click here

Creating a hyperlink to a Web or Intranet HTML file

Select the text or graphic you want to be the source of the link. Pull down the Insert menu and do the following:

 To amend a document hyperlink, place the insertion point within it (for text hyperlinks) or select the picture (for picture hyperlinks). Follow steps 1-2. In step 3, make the necessary changes. Finally, carry out step 4.

Click here

2 Click Existing File or Web Page

 To delete a document hyperlink, place the insertion point within it (for text hyperlinks) or select the picture (for picture hyperlinks). Follow steps 1-2. Now click this button:

Remove Link

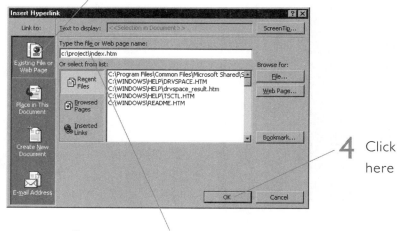

4 Click here

3 Type in a document address

Activating hyperlinks

To jump to one of the following:

- a bookmark (see page 56)

- a linked World Wide Web or Intranet document

do the following:

To activate a hyperlink to a World Wide Web document, first ensure your Internet connection is live.

Here, a hyperlink to Computer Step's Web site (http://www.ineasysteps.com) is being activated – notice that the mouse pointer changes to a hand

When you activate a hyperlink to a Web or Intranet document, Word 2000 opens a read-only version of it.

Click any hyperlink (inserted text hyperlinks are underlined and coloured blue)

Undo and redo

Word lets you reverse – 'undo' – just about any editing operation. If, subsequently, you decide that you do want to proceed with an operation that you've reversed, you can 'redo' it.

You can even undo or redo a series of operations in one go.

You can undo and redo actions in the following ways (in descending order of complexity):

- via the keyboard

- from within the Edit menu

- from within the Standard toolbar

Using the keyboard

Simply press Ctrl+Z to undo an action, or Ctrl+Y to reinstate it.

Using the Edit menu

Pull down the Edit menu and click Undo... or Redo... as appropriate (the ellipses denote the precise nature of the action to be reversed or reinstated).

Using the Standard toolbar

Carry out the following action to undo an action (see the DON'T FORGET tip for how to reinstate it):

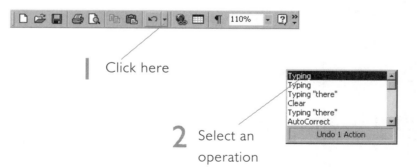

Click here

2 Select an operation

Text styles – an overview

The basic template also has a number of Internet-related styles e.g.:

- HTML Address
- HTML Keyboard, and;
- HTML Sample

These styles use Times New Roman or Courier as their base typefaces, and are particularly suitable for use in Web documents.

Styles are named collections of associated formatting commands.

The advantage of using styles is that you can apply more than one formatting enhancement to selected text in one go. Once a style is in place, you can change one or more elements of it and have Word 2000 apply the amendments automatically throughout the whole of the active document.

Generally, new documents you create in Word 2000 are based on the NORMAL.DOT template and have a variety of pre-defined styles. Some of the main ones include:

Body Text	used for specialised body text
Body Text 1	used for specialised body text
Body Text 2	used for specialised body text
Normal	used for standard body text
Default Paragraph Text	used for paragraph text
Heading 1	used for headings
Heading 2	used for headings
Heading 3	used for headings
Heading 4	used for headings
Heading 5	used for headings
Heading 6	used for headings
Heading 7	used for headings
Heading 8	used for headings
Heading 9	used for headings
Hyperlink	used to denote inactivated hyperlinks

You can easily create (and apply) your own styles – see pages 63-64.

There are also more specialised styles in NORMAL.DOT. These relate to:

- generic, bulleted and numbered lists
- titles and subtitles
- page numbers, and;
- hyperlinks which have been clicked (activated)

Finding out which text style is in force

If you're in any doubt about which style is associated with text, you can arrange to view style names in a special pane to the left of text.

Pull down the Tools menu and click Options. Do the following:

You can only view the Style pane in Normal view.

Activate this tab

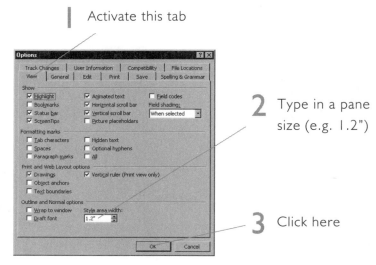

Re step 2 – if you no longer wish to view the Style Pane, reset the pane size to 0".

2 Type in a pane size (e.g. 1.2")

3 Click here

To view the Style pane, pull down the View menu and click Normal (if Normal view isn't already active):

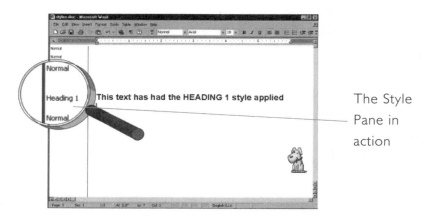

The Style Pane in action

Creating a text style

The easiest way to create a style is to:

A.   apply the appropriate formatting enhancements to specific text and then select it

B.   tell Word to save this formatting as a style

First, carry out A. above. Then pull down the Format menu and click Style. Now do the following:

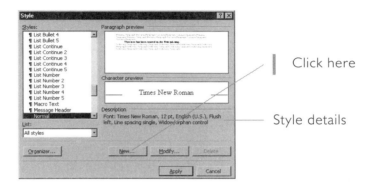

Click here

Style details

By default, Word 2000 applies the following names to new styles: 'Style 1', 'Style 2' etc.

2 Name the new style

Brief description of formatting associated with the new style

3 Click here

See page 64 for how to use your new style.

Applying a text style

Word 2000 makes applying styles easy.

First, select the text you want to apply the style to. Or, if you only want to apply it to a single paragraph, place the insertion point inside it. Pull down the Format menu and click Style. Now do the following:

You can delete user-created styles, if necessary.
Follow step 1. Click the Delete button. In the message which launches, click Yes. Finally, click the Close button.
(When you delete a style, any text associated with it automatically has the Normal style applied to it.)

Click a style

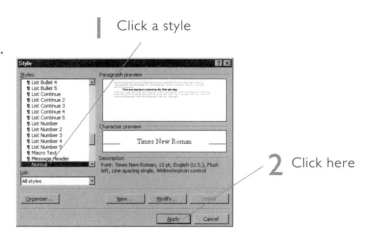

2 Click here

Shortcut for applying styles

Word 2000 makes it even easier to apply styles if you currently have the Formatting toolbar on-screen. (If you haven't, pull down the View menu and click Toolbars, Formatting.)

Re the shortcut – if you've used the Style button before, Word 2000 may have promoted it to the main body of the Formatting toolbar.

Select the text you want to apply the style to. Click » in the Formatting toolbar then do the following:

Click here in the Style button

Re step 2 – entries in the Style drop-down list display with accurate formatting.

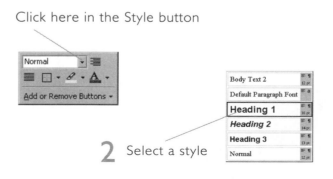

2 Select a style

Amending a text style

The easiest way to modify an existing style is to:

A.   apply the appropriate formatting enhancements to specific text and then select it

Re step 1 – if you've used the Style button before, Word 2000 may have promoted it to the main body of the Formatting toolbar.

B.   use the Formatting toolbar to tell Word 2000 to assign the selected formatting to the associated style

First, carry out A. above. Click ⏶ in the Formatting toolbar, then do the following:

| Click here in the Style button

You can have Word 2000 update a style automatically whenever you amend the formatting of text to which it has been applied.

Pull down the Format menu and click Style. In the Styles field, select a style. Click this button:

In the Modify Style dialog, ensure Automatically update is selected. Click OK. Back in the Style dialog, click Apply or Close, as appropriate.

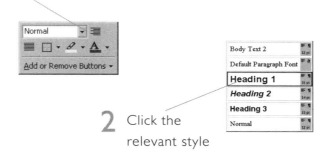

2   Click the relevant style

Word 2000 launches a special message. Do the following:

3   Make sure this is selected

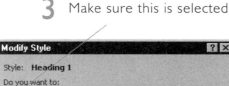
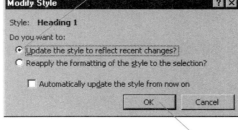

4   Click here to apply the specified amendments to the style

Spell- and grammar-checking

By default, Word 2000 checks spelling and grammar simultaneously.

Word 2000 lets you check text in two ways:

- on-the-fly, as you type in text

- separately, after the text has been entered

Checking text on-the-fly

This is the default. When automatic checking is in force, Word 2000 flags words it doesn't agree with a red underline (in the case of misspellings) and a green line (for grammatical errors). If the word or phrase is wrong, right-click in it. Then carry out steps 1, 2 or 3:

Re step 2 – if Word has flagged a spelling error, you have an extra option. C lick Add if:

- *the flagged word is correct, and;*

- *you want Word to remember it in future spell-checks (by adding it to your User dictionary)*

1 Word often provides a list of alternatives. If one is correct, click it; the flagged word is replaced with the correct version

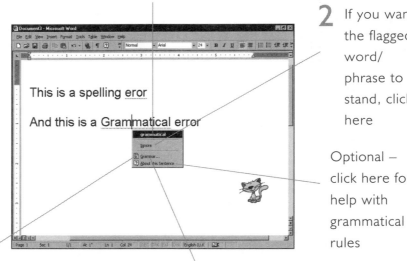

2 If you want the flagged word/ phrase to stand, click here

Optional – click here for help with grammatical rules

Here, we're correcting a grammatical error. If a spelling error has been flagged, this section of the menu shows:

3 If the flagged word is wrong but can't be corrected now, click here and complete the resulting dialog (see over)

Disabling on-the-fly checking

Pull down the Tools menu and click Options. Activate the Spelling & Grammar tab, then deselect Check spelling as you type and/or Check grammar as you type. Click OK.

Checking text separately

To check all the text within the active document in one go, pull down the Tools menu and click Spelling and Grammar. Word 2000 starts spell- and grammar-checking the document from the beginning. When it encounters a word or phrase it doesn't recognise, Word flags it and produces a special dialog (see below). Usually, it provides alternative suggestions; if one of these is correct, you can opt to have it replace the flagged word. You can do this singly (i.e. just this instance is replaced) or globally (where all future instances – within the current checking session – are replaced).

Alternatively, you can have Word ignore *this* instance of the flagged word, ignore *all* future instances of the word or add the word to CUSTOM.DIC (see the tips). After this, Word resumes checking.

Carry out step 1 below, then follow step 2. Alternatively, carry out step 3 or 4.

Word makes use of two separate dictionaries. One – CUSTOM.DIC – is yours. When you click the Add button (see the tip below), the flagged word is stored in CUSTOM.DIC and recognised in future checking sessions.

If you're correcting a spelling error, you have two further options:

- *Click Add to have the flagged word stored in CUSTOM.DIC (see above), or;*
- *Click Change All to have Word substitute its suggestion for all future instances of the flagged word*

Word's Word Assistant explains basic grammatical points here.

1 If one of the suggestions here is correct, click it, then follow step 2

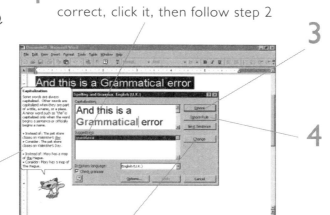

3 Click here to ignore just this instance

4 Click here to ignore all future instances

2 Click here to replace this instance

Searching for synonyms

Word 2000 lets you search for synonyms while you're editing the active document. You do this by calling up Word's resident Thesaurus. The Thesaurus categorises words into meanings; each meaning is allocated various synonyms from which you can choose.

As a bonus, the Thesaurus also supplies antonyms. For example, if you look up 'good' in the Thesaurus (as below), Word lists 'poor' as an antonym.

Word 2000's Thesaurus may not be installed (Install on Demand in action).

If it isn't, follow the on-screen instructions after clicking Language, Thesaurus in the Tools menu.

Using the thesaurus

First, select the word for which you require a synonym or antonym (or simply position the insertion point within it). Pull down the Tools menu and click Language, Thesaurus. Now do the following:

The selected word appears here

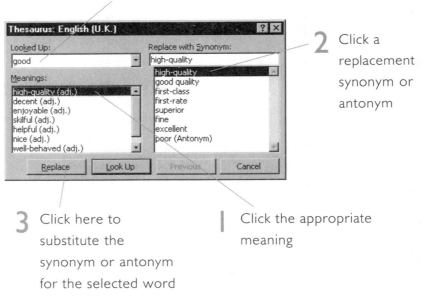

2 Click a replacement synonym or antonym

3 Click here to substitute the synonym or antonym for the selected word

1 Click the appropriate meaning

Working with pictures

Word 2000 lets you add colour and greyscale pictures to the active document. Pictures – also called graphics – include:

- drawings produced in other programs

- clip art

- scanned photographs

Pictures are stored in various third-party formats. These formats are organised into two basic types:

Bitmap images

Bitmaps consist of pixels (dots) arranged in such a way that they form a graphic image. Because of the very nature of bitmaps, the question of 'resolution' – the sharpness of an image expressed in dpi (dots per inch) – is very important. Bitmaps look best if they're displayed at their correct resolution. Word 2000 can manipulate a wide variety of third-party bitmap graphics formats. These include: PCX, TIF, TGA and GIF.

Vector images

You can also insert vector graphics files into Word 2000 documents. Vector images consist of and are defined by algebraic equations. They're less complex than bitmaps and contain less detail. Vector files can also include bitmap information.

Irrespective of the format type, Word 2000 can incorporate pictures with the help of special 'filters'. These are special mini-programs whose job it is to translate third-party formats into a form which Word can use.

You can have Word 2000 insert pictures automatically, by using its AutoCorrect feature.

To set up a picture as an AutoCorrect entry, select it. Pull down the Tools menu and click AutoCorrect. In the Replace field, insert the word/phrase you want the picture to replace. Select Formatted text. Click Add, followed by OK.

To insert a picture stored as an AutoCorrect entry, do the following:

- *type in the verbal trigger you set in the HOT TIP above, then;*

- *press Space (or any other punctuation mark e.g. a comma or full stop). Alternatively, press Enter or Return*

Brief notes on picture formats

Graphics formats Word 2000 will accept include the following (the column on the left shows the file suffix):

Additional formats include (both are used on the World Wide Web):

BMP A popular bitmap format

JPEG *Joint Photographic Experts Group. Used on the PC and Mac for storing photographs. Can be used in HTML files. Incorporates very high compression*

CGM Computer Graphics Metafile. A vector format frequently used in the past, especially as a medium for clip-art transmission. Less often used nowadays.

EPS Encapsulated PostScript. Perhaps the most widely used PostScript format. PostScript combines vector *and* bitmap data very successfully. Incorporates a low-resolution bitmap 'header' for preview purposes.

PNG *Portable Network Graphics. Incorporates high compression but not all browsers can handle it*

GIF Graphics Interchange Format. Developed for the on-line transmission of graphics data over the Internet. Just about any Windows program – and a lot more besides – will read GIF. Disadvantage: it can't handle more than 256 colours. Compression is supported.

PCD (Kodak) PhotoCD. Used primarily to store photographs on CD.

PCX An old stand-by. Originated with PC Paintbrush, a paint program. Used for years to transfer graphics data between Windows applications.

Compression makes graphics occupy less space on disk.

TGA Targa. A high-end format, and also a bridge with so-called low-end computers (e.g. Amiga and Atari). Often used in PC and Mac paint and ray-tracing programs because of its high-resolution colour fidelity.

TIFF Tagged Image File Format. Suffix: TIF. If anything, even more widely used than PCX, across a whole range of platforms and applications.

WMF A frequently used vector format. Used for information exchange between just about all Windows programs

Inserting pictures

You can use Click and Type to insert pictures in blank page areas – see pages 28-29.

You can insert pictures in two ways:

* with the Word Clip Gallery

* using a separate dialog

Inserting pictures via the Clip Gallery

First, position the insertion point at the location within the active document where you want to insert the picture. Pull down the Insert menu and click Picture, Clip Art. Do the following:

All clips have associated keywords. You can use these to locate clips. Click in this field in the Gallery:

| Type one or more words... |

Now type in one or more keywords. Finally, press Enter – any relevant clips display.

Re step 2 – the Clip Gallery organises clips under overall categories.

Ensure this tab is activated

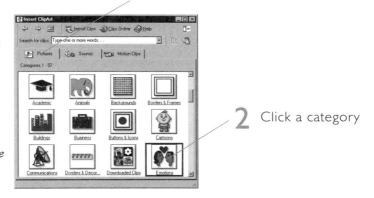

2 Click a category

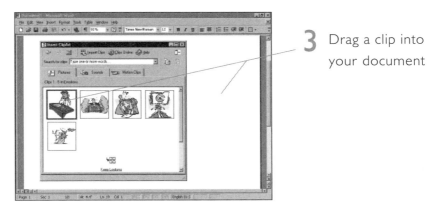

3 Drag a clip into your document

4 Release the mouse button – Word 2000 inserts the picture

*You can use
Click and Type
to insert
pictures in
blank page
areas – see pages 28-29.*

Inserting pictures – the dialog route

First, position the insertion point at the location within the
active document where you want to insert the picture. Pull
down the Insert menu and do the following:

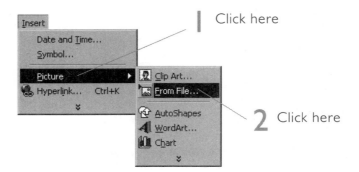

| Click here

2 Click here

4 Click here. In the drop-down list, click the
drive/folder that hosts the picture

*Word 2000
provides a
preview of what
the picture will
look like when
it's been imported.
(See the Preview box on
the right of the dialog.)*

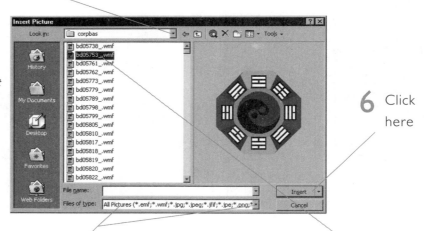

6 Click
here

3 Make sure All Pictures... is
shown. If it isn't, click the
arrow and select it from the
drop-down list

5 Click a
picture file

Editing pictures

Once you've inserted pictures into a Word 2000 document, you can amend them in a variety of ways. For instance, you can:

- rescale them

- apply a border

- crop them

- move them

To carry out any of these operations, you have to select the relevant picture first. To do this, simply position the mouse pointer over the image and left-click once. Word surrounds the image with eight handles. These are positioned at the four corners, and midway on each side. The illustration below demonstrates these:

If an image's handles display as closed boxes, this means that it can't be moved.

To rectify this, right-click the image. In the menu, select Format Picture. In the Format Picture dialog, click the Layout tab. Select a wrapping style other than In line with text (e.g. Square). Click OK.

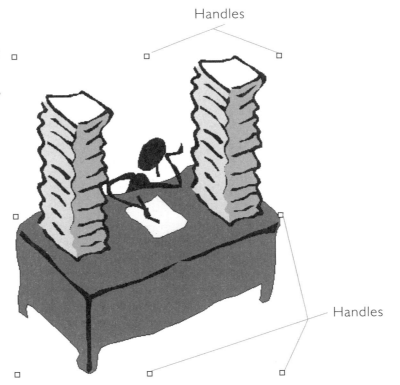

Handles

Handles

Rescaling pictures

There are two ways in which you can rescale pictures:

- proportionally, where the height/width ratio remains constant

- disproportionately, where the height/width ratio is disrupted (this is sometimes called 'warping' or 'skewing')

To rescale a picture, first select it. Then move the mouse pointer over:

- one of the corner handles, if you want to rescale the image proportionately, or;

- one of the handles in the middle of the sides, if you want to warp it

In either eventuality, the mouse pointer changes to a double-headed arrow. Click and hold down the left mouse button. Drag outwards to increase the image size or inwards to decrease it. Release the mouse button to confirm the change.

To move a picture on the page, select it (but first see the tip on page 73). Then move the mouse pointer over the picture. Click and hold down the left mouse button; drag the image to a new location. Release the mouse button to confirm the move.

To control how text aligns around a picture, select it. Pull down the Format menu and click Picture. In the Format Picture dialog, activate the Layout tab. Now select a text wrap option e.g.:

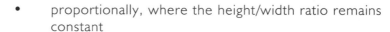

where text aligns around the top and bottom of the image, but not the sides. Finally, click OK.

Here, the image has been skewed to the right

Bordering pictures

By default, Word 2000 does not apply a border to inserted pictures. However, you can apply a wide selection of borders if you want. You can specify:

- the style and/or thickness of the border
- the border colour
- whether the border is dashed

Applying a border

First, select the picture you want to border. Then pull down the Format menu and click Borders and Shading. Now carry out step 1 below. Perform 2-5, as appropriate. Finally, carry out step 6:

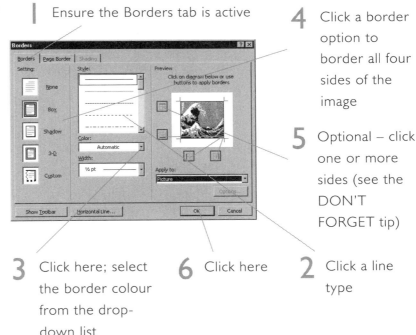

1 Ensure the Borders tab is active

4 Click a border option to border all four sides of the image

5 Optional – click one or more sides (see the DON'T FORGET tip)

3 Click here; select the border colour from the drop-down list

6 Click here

2 Click a line type

Cropping pictures

Cropping is the process of trimming the edges from a picture, either to make it fit within a smaller space or to remove parts that are unwanted.

Cropping a picture

First, select the picture you want to crop. Then refer to the Picture toolbar. (If it isn't visible, pull down the View menu and click Toolbars, Picture). Do the following:

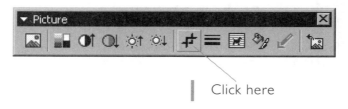

Click here

Now select the picture you want to crop. Move the mouse pointer over one of the available eight handles. Hold down the left mouse button and drag the handle inwards. Release the button to confirm the cropping operation.

Note that when you've carried out step 1, the pointer becomes:

Here, the image has been cropped using the centre right handle

Additional features – an overview

Word 2000 provides the following extra features which are designed to enhance and/or speed up the way you work:

Quick File Switching This allows you to switch to open documents more easily and conveniently

Problem correction Word 2000 identifies and corrects a wide variety of problems

Install on Demand You can install only those features you want to use at the moment – other features can easily be installed later, when required

Themes (not all may be pre-installed) are an example of Install on Demand – see the illustration.

Collect and Paste You can now copy and store as many as 12 items of text and/or pictures, and then paste them into Word 2000 documents at will

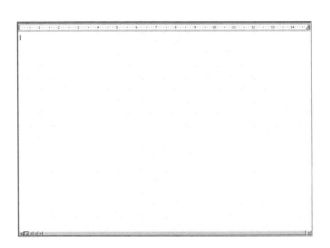

A theme applied to a Word file – see page 80

Quick File Switching

In the past, only programs (not individual windows within programs) displayed on the Windows Taskbar. With Word 2000, however, all open windows display as separate buttons.

In the following example, four new documents have been created in Word 2000. All four display as separate windows, although only one copy of Word 2000 is running:

4 Word 2000 windows

This is clarified by a glance at Word 2000's Window menu which shows all open Word windows:

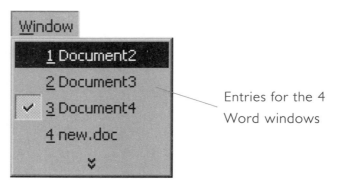

Entries for the 4 Word windows

Use this technique to go to a Word 2000 window by simply clicking its Taskbar button, a considerable saving in time and effort.

Repairing errors

Word 2000 provides the following:

Automatic repair

Whenever you launch Word 2000, it:

1.   determines if essential files are missing or corrupted

2.   automatically reinstalls the files

3.   repairs incorrect entries (relating to missing or corrupted files) in the Windows Registry

Manual repair

There are other potential problems which, though far less serious, can still result in lost productivity – e.g. corrupted fonts and missing templates.

Word 2000 has a special diagnostic procedure (called 'Detect and Repair') which you can run when necessary. The procedure:

1.   scrutinises the original state of your installation

2.   compares this with the present state of your installation

3.   takes the appropriate remedial steps

To run Detect and Repair in Word 2000, pull down the Help menu and do the following:

After step 1, complete any dialogs which launch.

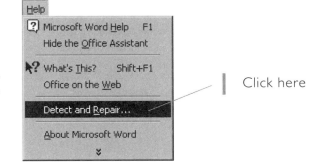

Click here

Word 2000 now detects and remedies any problem – this process may take some time.

Install on Demand

Word 2000 makes use of a new feature which allows users to install program components on demand, only when they're needed. However, the following display within Word 2000:

- shortcuts

- icons

- menu entries

for the uninstalled features.

An example of Install on Demand is themes. During installation, only a restricted number of themes may be copied to the user's hard disk. When you attempt to apply a theme which hasn't been installed, you're invited to rectify this.

Do the following:

To add an already installed theme to a Word file, click Theme in the Format menu. In the Choose a Theme: field, select a field. Click OK.

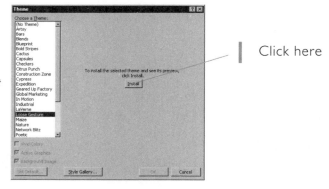

Click here

Networked users may be asked to refer to a specific server location instead...

2 After a pause, a further dialog may appear. If so, insert the relevant CD and click OK.

Collect and Paste

Collect and Paste uses a special Clipboard which is exclusive to Word 2000. Up to 12 items can be stored in it at the same time.

In previous versions of Word, if you wanted to copy-and-paste multiple items of text and/or pictures into a document, it was necessary (since the Windows Clipboard can only hold one item at a time) to perform each operation separately. Now, however, with Word 2000 you can use the new Collect and Paste operation to make this much easier.

Using Collect and Paste

From within Word 2000, use standard procedures to copy multiple examples of text and/or pictures – after the second copy, the Clipboard Toolbar launches. Now do the following:

If the Clipboard toolbar doesn't appear, do the following. Select and copy the same item of text (or a picture) twice.

The Clipboard Toolbar – in the top row, all four words have been copied, while the bottom row shows the copied picture

To clear the contents of the Word 2000 Clipboard, click this button:

in the toolbar.

You can copy multiple items to the Word Clipboard from within any Windows program which supports copy-and-paste, but you can only paste in the last one.

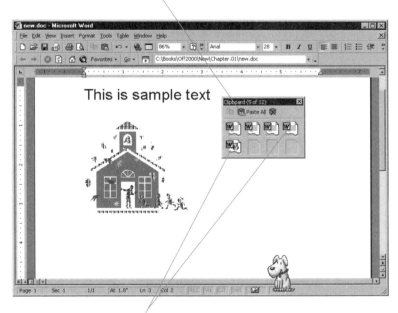

2 Click an icon to paste in the contents

Page setup – an overview

You can control page layout to a great extent in Word 2000. You can specify:

- the top, bottom, left and/or right page margins

- the distance between the top page edge and the top edge of the header

- the distance between the bottom page edge and bottom edge of the footer

The illustration below shows these page components:

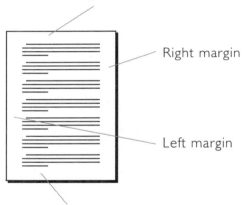

Top margin (including header)

Right margin

Left margin

Bottom margin (including footer)

You can also specify:

- the page size (irrespective of margins and headers/footers)

- the page orientation ('landscape' or 'portrait')

If none of the supplied page sizes is suitable, you can even customise your own.

Specifying margins

Margin settings are the framework on which indents and tabs are based.

All documents have margins, because printing on the whole of a sheet is both unsightly and – in the case of many printers, since the mechanism has to grip the page – impossible. Documents need a certain amount of 'white space' (the unprinted portion of the page) to balance the areas which contain text and graphics. Without this, they can't be visually effective. As a result, it's important to set margins correctly.

Customising margins

First, position the insertion point at the location within the active document from which you want the new margin(s) to apply. Alternatively, select the relevant portion of your document. Then pull down the File menu and click Page Setup. Now carry out step 1 below. Then follow steps 2-5, as appropriate. Finally, carry out step 6.

1 Ensure the Margins tab is active

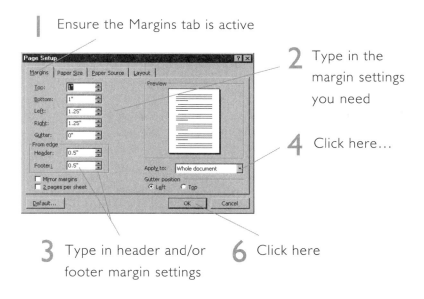

2 Type in the margin settings you need

4 Click here...

3 Type in header and/or footer margin settings

6 Click here

Re step 5 – if you selected text before launching this dialog, click
Selected Text.

5 Then specify how much of the document you want the new margin(s) to affect

Specifying the page size

Word 2000 comes with some 17 preset page sizes – for instance, A4, A5 and Letter. These are suitable for most purposes. However, you can also set up your own page definition if you need to.

Whatever the page size, you can have both portrait and landscape pages in the same document.

There are two aspects to every page size: a vertical measurement, and a horizontal measurement. These can be varied according to orientation. There are two possible orientations:

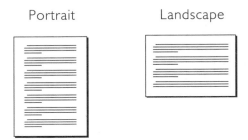

Portrait   Landscape

Setting the page size

First, position the insertion point at the location within the active document from which you want the new page size to apply. Then pull down the File menu and click Page Setup. Now do the following:

Re step 2 – to create your own page size, click Custom size. Then type in the desired measurements in the Width and Height fields. Finally, carry out step 4.

If you don't want your changes to affect the entire document, click the Apply to: field. In the list, select a more appropriate option (e.g. This point forward). Finally, perform step 4.

1 Ensure the Paper Size tab is active

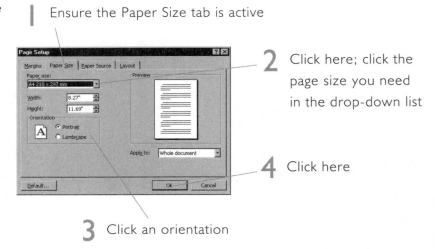

2 Click here; click the page size you need in the drop-down list

4 Click here

3 Click an orientation

Using Print Preview

You can edit text directly from within Print Preview. With the magnifying cursor displaying, zoom in on the text you want to edit (see page 86 for how to do this). Click this button in the Print Preview toolbar:

The cursor becomes:

Now click in the text and make the necessary changes.

To leave Print Preview mode, simply press Esc.

Word 2000 provides a special view mode called Print Preview. This displays the active document exactly as it will look when printed. Use Print Preview as a final check just before you print your document.

You can customise the way Print Preview displays your document in various ways. For example, you can:

- zoom in or out on the active page

- specify how many pages display

- hide almost everything on screen apart from the document

Launching Print Preview

Pull down the File menu and click Print Preview. This is the result:

Print Preview toolbar

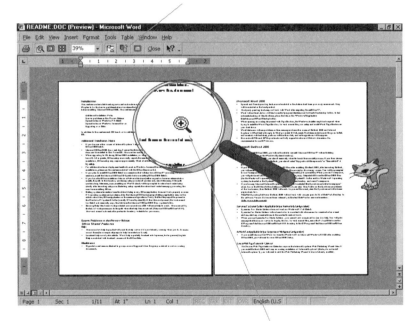

Magnifying cursor – see page 86

Zooming in or out in Print Preview

There are two ways in which you can change the display magnification in Print Preview mode.

Using the mouse

If you've just launched Print Preview, the Magnifier cursor will already be on-screen.

By default, the cursor in Print Preview is a magnifying glass – see the illustration on page 85 for what it looks like. You can use this to magnify *part* of the active document.

If the cursor currently isn't a magnifying glass, do the following in the Print Preview toolbar:

Click here

Now position the Magnifier cursor over the portion of the active document that you want to expand. Left-click once.

Using the Zoom Control button

To choose from pre-defined Zoom sizes, do the following:

Click here

Using the Zoom Control button affects the whole of the active document.

2 Click a new Zoom option

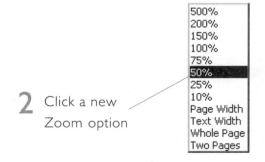

Multiple pages in Print Preview

In Print Preview mode, you can view as many as twenty-four (3 x 8) pages at the same time.

Turn to the Print Preview toolbar and do the following:

Click here

Word launches a graphical list:

Word tells you here what page permutation you've chosen, e.g. '1 x 2' (2 pages displayed at full size), or '2 x 1' (2 pages displayed as thumbnails).

Click and hold here, then follow the instructions below

Position the mouse pointer over the first icon (see the illustration above). Hold down the left mouse button. Drag the pointer to the right and/or down (the list expands as you do so). When you find the right page multiple, release the mouse button.

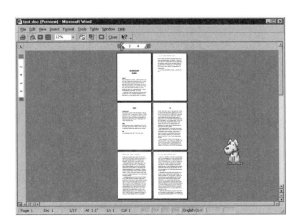

3 x 2 view

Clearing the screen in Print Preview

We saw earlier that it's possible to hide superfluous screen components in Normal, Web Layout and Print Layout views. You can also do this in Print Preview mode. Word calls this Full Screen view.

Even the Word Assistant disappears off-screen.

The advantage is that using Full Screen view in Print Preview mode makes even more space available for display purposes. This is highly desirable unless you have a particularly large monitor. In Print Preview mode, Full Screen view hides all screen components with the exception of the Print Preview toolbar and the dedicated Full Screen toolbar.

Implementing Full Screen view

Refer to the Print Preview toolbar and do the following:

Click here

To leave Full Screen view, repeat this procedure.

You can use the following shortcuts to leave Full Screen view:

- *simply press Esc*

- *alternatively, click here:*

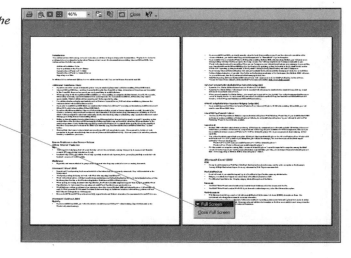

1 x 2 pages in Full Screen view

Printer setup

Most Word 2000 documents need to be printed eventually. Before you can begin printing, however, you need to ensure that:

- the correct printer is selected (if you have more than one installed)

- the correct printer settings are in force

Word 2000 calls these collectively the 'printer setup'.

Irrespective of the printer selected, the settings vary in accordance with the job in hand. For example, most printer drivers (the software which 'drives' the printer) allow you to specify whether or not you want pictures printed. Additionally, they often allow you to specify the resolution or print quality of the output...

Selecting the printer and/or settings

At any time before you're ready to print a document, pull down the File menu and click Print. Now do the following:

Click here; select the printer you want from the list

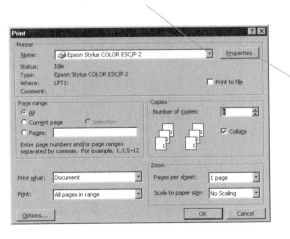

2 Click here to adjust printer settings (see your printer's manual for how to do this)

Now complete the remainder of the Print dialog, prior to printing your document (see pages 92-93).

Printing – an overview

Once the active document is how you want it (and you've customised the printer setup appropriately), you'll probably need to print it out. Word 2000 makes this process easy and straightforward. It lets you set a variety of options before you do so.

Alternatively, you can simply opt to print your document with the current settings in force (Word 2000 provides a 'fast track' approach to this).

Available print options include:

- the number of copies you want printed

- whether you want the copies 'collated'. This is the process whereby Word 2000 prints one full copy at a time. For instance, if you're printing three copies of a 40-page document, Word prints pages 1-40 of the first document, followed by pages 1-40 of the second and pages 1-40 of the third.

- which pages (or page ranges) you want printed

- whether you want to limit the print run to odd or even pages

- whether you want the print run restricted to text you selected before initiating printing

- whether you want the pages printed in reverse order (e.g. from the last page to the first)

- the quality of the eventual output (with many printers, Word 2000 allows you to print with minimal formatting for proofing purposes)

- whether you want to go on working in Word 2000 while the document prints (the default). Word 2000 calls this 'background printing'

You can 'mix and match' these, as appropriate.

Printing – the fast track approach

Since documents and printing needs vary dramatically, it's often necessary to customise print options before you begin printing. (See pages 92-93 for how to do this).

On the other hand, there are occasions when you'll merely want to print out your work:

• without having to invoke the Print dialog

• with the current settings applying

• with a single mouse click

You can also access fast-track printing from within Print Preview. Simply click this button:

in the Print Preview toolbar.

One reason for doing this is proofing. Irrespective of how thoroughly you check documents on-screen, there will always be errors and deficiencies which, with the best will in the world, are difficult or impossible to pick up. By initiating printing with the minimum of delay, you can check your work that much more rapidly...

For this reason, Word 2000 provides a printing method which is quicker and easier to use.

Printing with the current print options

First, ensure your printer is ready and on-line. Make sure the Standard toolbar is visible. (If it isn't, pull down the View menu and click Toolbars, Standard). Now do the following:

Click here

Word 2000 starts printing the active document immediately.

Customised printing

If you need to set revised print options before printing, do the following.

Pull down the File menu and click Print. Now carry out steps 1-5, as appropriate. Finally, carry out step 6.

For more options, carry out the actions on the facing page before you perform step 5 here.

To print only odd or even pages, click the Print field. Click Odd Pages or Even Pages.

To print more than one page on a sheet, click Pages per sheet. Select a number in the list.

Re step 3 – separate non-adjacent pages with commas but no spaces (and no comma at the end) – e.g. to print pages 5, 12, 16 and 19 type in:

5,12,16,19

Enter contiguous pages with dashes – e.g. to print pages 12 to 23 inclusive, type in:

12-23

1 Click here to deselect collation

2 Type in the number of copies

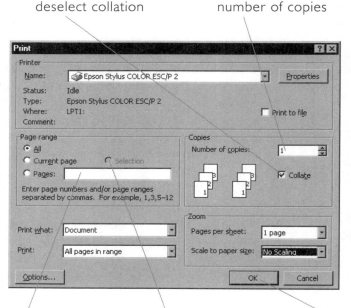

3 Type in the relevant page range (see tip opposite)

4 Click here if you selected text before launching this dialog and this is all you want to print

5 Click here

Word starts printing the active document.

Other print options are accessible from within a special dialog. This is launched from within the Print dialog.

First, pull down the File menu and click Print. Then do the following:

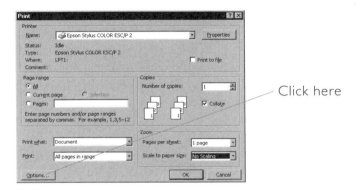

Click here

Now perform steps 1-3 below, as appropriate. Then follow step 4.

Ensure this is selected to print with minimal formatting

Re step 2 – if you want to speed up printing, deselect Background printing. (But note that if you do this, you won't be able to continue working until printing is complete.)

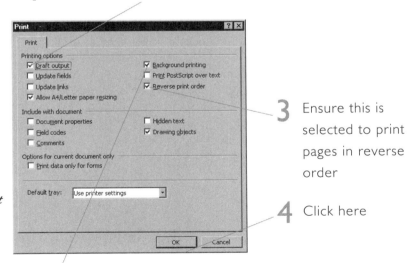

3 Ensure this is selected to print pages in reverse order

Step 4 returns you to the Print dialog. Now follow step 5 on the facing page to initiate printing.

4 Click here

2 Deselect this to turn off background printing

Word's Office Assistant

When you move the mouse pointer over toolbar buttons, Word launches an explanatory bubble called a ToolTip:

*You can also move the mouse pointer over fields in dialogs, commands or screen areas and produce a specific **HELP** box. To do this, right-click the field then left-click the What's This? menu.*

Word 2000 has a unique HELP feature which is designed to make it much easier to become productive: the Assistant. The Assistant:

- answers questions directly. This is an especially useful feature for the reason that, normally when you invoke a program's HELP system, you know more or less the question you want to ask, or the topic on which you need information. If neither of these is true, however, the Office Assistant responds to plain English questions and provides a choice of answers. For example, responses produced by entering 'What are ToolTips?' include:

  — *Show or hide shortcut keys in ToolTips*

  — *Show or hide toolbar ScreenTips*

  — *Rename a menu command or toolbar button*

- provides context-sensitive tips

- answers questions in your own words

The Assistant is animated. It can also change shape! To do this, click the Options button. In the dialog which appears, activate the Gallery tab. Click the Next button until the Assistant you want is displayed. Click OK, then follow any further on-screen instructions.

Word 2000's Assistant, after it has just launched

If the HELP bubble isn't displayed, simply click anywhere in the Assistant.

You can also use a keyboard shortcut to launch the Assistant.
Simply press F1.

Launching the Assistant

By default, the Assistant displays automatically. If it isn't currently on-screen, however, refer to the Standard toolbar and do the following:

Click here

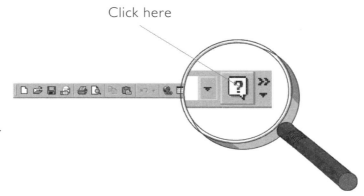

To close an Assistant window at any time, press Esc, or click the
Close button.

Hiding the Assistant

If you don't want the Office Assistant to display, right-click over it and do the following:

If you don't want to use the Assistant at all, click here:
In the Office Assistant dialog, activate the Options tab. Deselect Use the Office Assistant. Click OK.

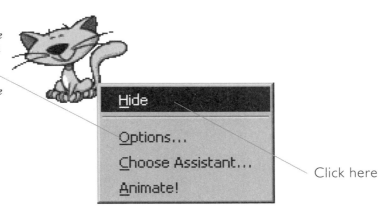

Click here

Spontaneous tips

Sometimes, the Assistant will indicate that it has a tip which may be useful:

As you'll have noticed, you can change the Assistant. For how to do this, see the HOT TIP on page 94.

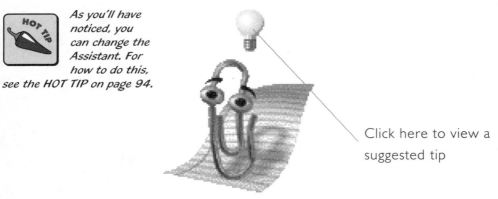

Click here to view a suggested tip

The tip launches. Do the following when you've finished with it:

To turn the Assistant back on after you've disabled it, pull down the Help menu and do the following:

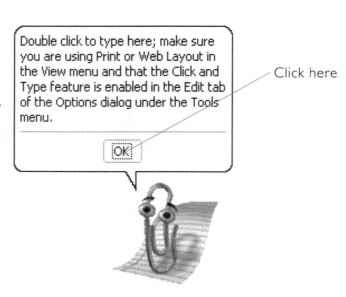

Click here

Click here

The Spreadsheet

This chapter gives you the basics of using the Spreadsheet module. You'll learn how to work with data and formulas, and how to move around in spreadsheets. You'll also discover how to locate data, and make it more visually effective by converting it to charts. Finally, you'll customise page layout/printing and use inbuilt HELP.

Covers

Chapter Three

The Spreadsheet screen

Below is a detailed illustration of the Spreadsheet screen.

Title bar   Menu bar   Column headings

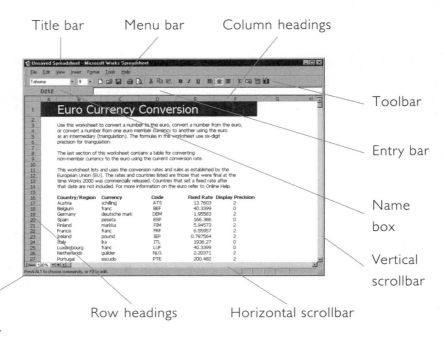

Toolbar

Entry bar

Name box

Vertical scrollbar

This is the Zoom Area: The screen components here are used to adjust magnification levels. See pages 105-106.

Row headings   Horizontal scrollbar

Some of these – e.g. the scrollbars – are standard to just about all programs which run under Windows. One – the Toolbar – can be hidden, if required.

Specifying whether the Toolbar displays

Pull down the View menu. Then do the following:

The tick signifies that the Toolbar is currently visible.

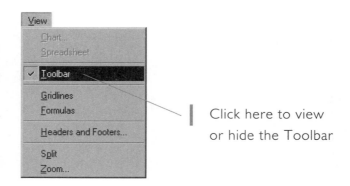

Click here to view or hide the Toolbar

Entering data

Columns are vertical, rows horizontal. Each spreadsheet can have as many as 256 columns and 16,384 rows, making a grand total of 4,194,304 cells.

You can insert the Euro symbol into spreadsheets. Fonts which support this include:

- *Arial*
- *Courier New*
- *Impact*
- *Tahoma, and;*
- *Times New Roman*

To insert the Euro symbol, press the Num Lock key on your keyboard. Hold down Alt and press 0128 (consecutively) on the numerical keypad. Release Alt and turn off Num Lock.

An inserted Euro symbol

When you start the Works Suite 2000 Spreadsheet module, you can use the Task Launcher to create a new blank spreadsheet (see Chapter 1 for how to do this). The result will look like this:

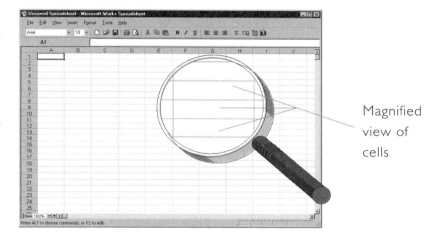

Magnified view of cells

This means that you can start entering data immediately.

In the Spreadsheet module, you can enter the following basic data types:

- values (i.e. numbers)

- text (e.g. headings and explanatory material)

- functions (e.g. Sine or Cosine)

- formulas (combinations of values, text and functions)

You enter data into 'cells'. Cells are formed where rows and columns intersect. In the most basic sense, collections of rows/columns and cells are known as spreadsheets.

Although you can enter data *directly* into a cell (by clicking in it, typing it in and pressing Enter), there's another method you can use which is often easier. The Spreadsheet provides a special screen component known as the Entry bar.

The illustration below shows the end of a blank spreadsheet. Some sample text has been inserted into cell IV16384 (note that the Name box tells you which cell is currently active):

Name box

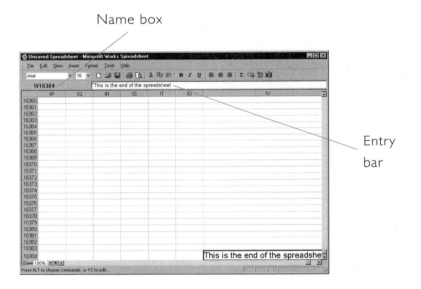

Entry bar

Entering data via the Entry bar

Click the cell you want to insert data into. Click the Entry bar. Type in the data. Then follow step 1 below. If you decide to cancel the operation, follow step 2 instead:

1 Click here

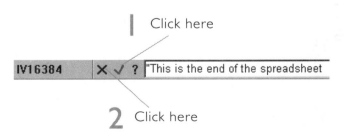

2 Click here

Modifying existing data

You can amend the contents of a cell in two ways:

- via the Entry bar

- from within the cell

When you use either of these methods, the Spreadsheet enters a special state known as Edit Mode.

Amending existing data using the Entry bar

Click the cell whose contents you want to change. Then click in the Entry bar. Make the appropriate revisions and/or additions. Then press Return. The relevant cell is updated.

Amending existing data internally

Click the cell whose contents you want to change. Press F2. Make the appropriate revisions and/or additions *within the cell*. Then press Return.

The illustration below shows a section of a spreadsheet created with the Financial Worksheets Wizard.

A magnified view of cell D15 in Edit Mode

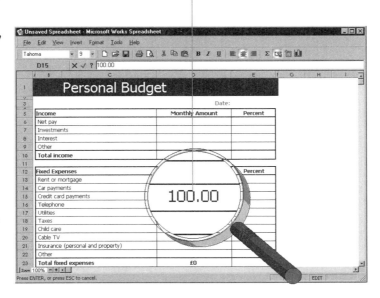

Working with cell ranges

When you're working with more than one cell, it's often convenient and useful to organise them in 'ranges'.

A range is a rectangular arrangement of cells. In the illustration below, cells B11, C11, D11, E11, F11, G11, B12, C12, D12, E12, F12 and G12 have been selected.

Gridlines

A selected cell range

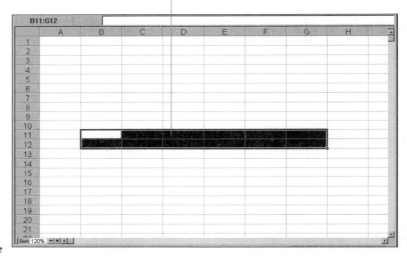

Cell 'shorthand'

The above description of the relevant cells is very cumbersome. It's much more useful to use a form of shorthand. The Spreadsheet module (using the start and end cells as reference points) refers to these cells as: B11:G12

This notation system makes it much easier to refer to sizeable cell ranges.

Moving around in spreadsheets

Spreadsheets can be huge. Moving to cells which happen currently to be visible is easy: you simply click in the relevant cell. However, the Spreadsheet module provides several techniques you can use to jump to less accessible areas.

Using the scrollbars

Use any of the following methods:

1. To scroll quickly to another section of the active spreadsheet, drag the scroll box along the scrollbar until you reach it

2. To move one window to the left or right, click to the left or right of the scroll box in the horizontal scrollbar

3. To move one window up or down, click above or below the scroll box in the vertical scrollbar

4. To move up or down by one row, click the arrows in the vertical scrollbar

5. To move left or right by one column, click the arrows in the horizontal scrollbar

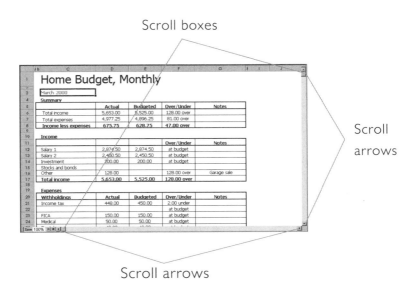

Scroll boxes

Scroll arrows

Scroll arrows

Using the keyboard

You can use the following techniques:

1. Use the cursor keys to move one cell left, right, up or down

2. Hold down Ctrl as you use 1. above; this jumps to the edge of the current section (e.g. if cell B11 is active and you hold down Ctrl as you press →, Works Suite 2000 jumps to IV11, the last cell in row 11)

3. Press Home to jump to the first cell in the active row, or Ctrl+Home to move to A1

4. Press Page Up or Page Down to move up or down by one screen

5. Press Ctrl+Page Down to move one screen to the right, or Ctrl+Page Up to move one screen to the left

You can use a keyboard shortcut to launch the Go To dialog.
Simply press F5, or Ctrl+G.

Using the Go To dialog

The Spreadsheet provides a special dialog which you can use to specify precise cell destinations.

Pull down the Edit menu and click Go To. Now do the following:

Re step 1 – a cell's 'reference' (or 'address') identifies it in relation to its position in a spreadsheet, e.g. B11 or H23.
You can also type in cell ranges here (e.g. B11:C15), or range names.

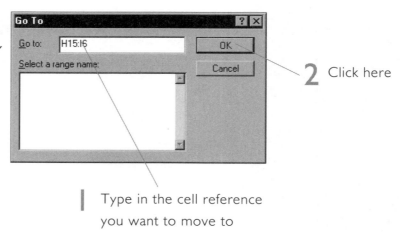

2 Click here

Type in the cell reference you want to move to

Changing Zoom levels

The ability to vary the level of magnification for the active document is especially useful for spreadsheets, which very often occupy more space than can be accommodated on-screen at any given time. Sometimes, it's helpful to 'zoom out' (i.e. decrease the magnification) so that you can take an overview; at other times, you'll need to 'zoom in' (increase the magnification) to work in greater detail.

You can alter magnification levels in the Spreadsheet module:

- with the use of the Zoom Area

- with the Zoom dialog

For more information on how to find the Zoom Area, see the illustration on page 98.

Using the Zoom Area

You can use the Zoom Area (at the base of the screen) to alter zoom levels with the minimum of effort. Carry out step 1 OR 2, or steps 3 AND 4, as appropriate:

Re step 4 – clicking Custom produces the Zoom dialog. (See overleaf for how to use this.)

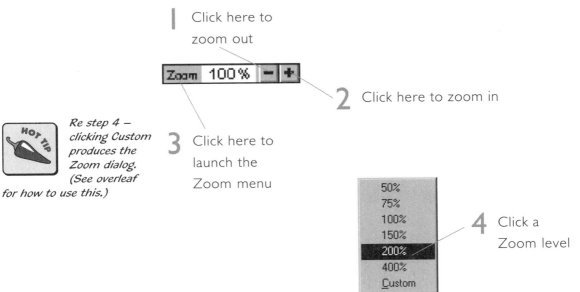

| Click here to zoom out

2 Click here to zoom in

3 Click here to launch the Zoom menu

4 Click a Zoom level

Using the Zoom dialog

Using the Zoom dialog, you can perform the following Zoom actions. You can:

Zoom settings have no effect on the way spreadsheets print.

- • choose from preset Zoom levels (e.g. 200%, 100%, 75%)

- • specify your own Zoom percentage

If you want to impose your own, custom zoom level, it's probably easier, quicker and more convenient to use the Zoom dialog.

Pull down the View menu and click Zoom. Now carry out step 1 or 2 below. Finally, follow step 3:

3 Click here

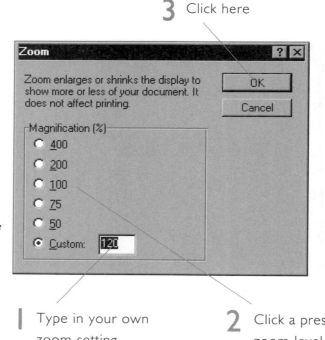

Re step 1 – entries must lie in the range 25%-1000%

1 Type in your own zoom setting

2 Click a preset zoom level

Selection techniques

Before you can carry out any editing operations on cells in the Spreadsheet module, you have to select them first. Selecting a single cell is very easy: you merely click in it. However, there are a variety of selection techniques which you can use to select more than one cell simultaneously.

Selecting cell ranges with the mouse

The easiest way to select more than one cell at a time is to use the mouse.

Click in the first cell in the range; hold down the left mouse button and drag over the remaining cells. Release the mouse button.

Selecting cell ranges with the keyboard

There are two separate techniques you can use:

With the exception of the first cell, a selected range is filled with

black.

- Position the cell pointer over the first cell in the range. Hold down one Shift key as you use the relevant cursor key to extend the selection. Release the keys when the correct selection has been defined

- Position the cell pointer over the first cell in the range. Press F8 to enter Selection mode. Use the cursor keys to define the selection area (see the illustration below). Finally, press F8 again to leave Selection mode

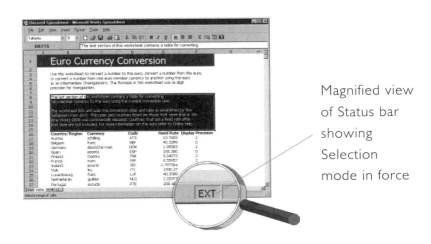

Magnified view
of Status bar
showing
Selection
mode in force

Selecting a single row or column

To select every cell within a row or column automatically, click the row or column heading.

Column heading

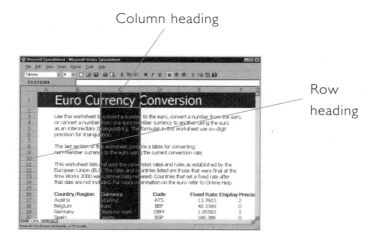

Row heading

Selecting multiple rows or columns

To select more than one row or column, click the row or column heading. Hold down the left mouse button and drag to select adjacent rows or columns.

You can use a keyboard shortcut to select every cell automatically. Simply press Ctrl+A, or Ctrl+Shift+F8.

Selecting an entire spreadsheet

Click the Select All button:

A magnified view of the Select All button

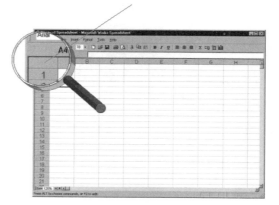

Formulas – an overview

Formulas are cell entries which define how other values relate to each other.

As a very simple example, consider the following:

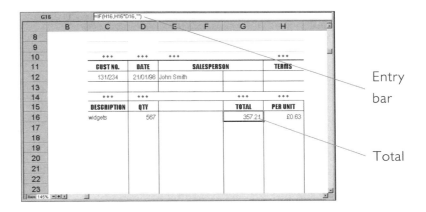

Entry bar

Total

Cell G16 has been defined so that it multiplies the contents of cells D16 and H16. Obviously, in this instance you could insert the result easily enough yourself because the values are so small, and because we're only dealing with a small number of cells. But what happens if the cell values are larger and/or more numerous, or – more to the point – if they're liable to change frequently?

The answer is to insert a formula which carries out the necessary calculation automatically.

*The 'H16*D16' component tells Works Suite 2000 to multiply the contents of the two cells. The 'IF' before the bracket is the conditional operator.*

If you look at the Entry bar in the illustration, you'll see the formula which does this:

=IF(HI6,HI6*DI6,"")

This is a fairly complex formula. Basically, it instructs Works Suite 2000 to inspect cell H16. If an entry is found, the contents should be multiplied by the contents of D16, and the results displayed.

Inserting a formula

Arguments (e.g. cell references) relating to functions are always contained in brackets.

All formulas in the Spreadsheet begin with an equals sign. This is usually followed by a permutation of the following:

- an operand (cell reference, e.g. B4)

- a function (e.g. the summation function, SUM)

- an arithmetical operator (+, −, /, * and ^)

- comparison operators (=, <, >, <=, >= and <>)

The Spreadsheet supports a very wide range of functions organised into numerous categories. For more information on how to insert functions, see the facing page.

The mathematical operators are (in the order in which they appear in the bulleted list): *plus, minus, divide, multiply* and *exponential*.

The comparison operators are (in the order in which they appear in the list): *equals, less than, greater than, less than or equal to, greater than or equal to* and *not equal to*.

There are two ways to enter formulas:

Entering a formula directly into the cell
Click the cell in which you want to insert a formula. Then type =, followed by your formula. When you've finished, press Return.

Entering a formula into the Entry bar

Using the Entry bar method is usually the most convenient.

Click the cell in which you want to insert a formula. Then click in the Entry bar. Type =, followed by your formula. When you've finished, press Return or do the following in the Entry bar:

Click here

Functions – an overview

Functions are pre-defined, built-in tools which accomplish specific tasks and then display the result. These tasks are very often calculations; occasionally, however, they're considerably more generalised (e.g. some functions simply return dates and/or times). In effect, functions replace one or more formulas.

The Spreadsheet module organises its functions under the following headings:

- Financial

- Date and Time

- Math and Trig

- Statistical

- Lookup and Ref

- Text

- Logical

- Informational

Works Suite 2000 provides a special shortcut (called Easy Calc) which makes entering functions much easier and more straightforward. Easy Calc is very useful for the following reasons:

— It provides access to a large number of functions from a centralised source

— It ensures that functions are entered with the correct syntax

Functions can only be used in formulas. Note, however, that the result displays in the host cell, rather than the underlying function/formula.

You can, however, have Works Suite 2000 display formulas/ functions in situ within the spreadsheet. Simply pull down the View menu and click Formulas.

Formulas showing in cells

(To re-hide formulas, repeat the above.)

Using Easy Calc

Inserting a function with Easy Calc

At the relevant juncture during the process of inserting a formula, pull down the Tools menu and click Easy Calc. Now carry out step 1 OR 2 below:

If you follow step 2, Works Suite 2000 launches the Insert Function dialog. Pick a function category in the Category field, then select the relevant function in the Choose a function box. Click Insert.
Now follow steps 3-6.

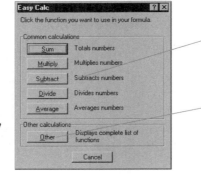

1 Click the appropriate function type

2 Click Other if you need an unusual function

Now complete the following dialogs (the contents vary with the function selected):

Re step 3 – click the cells (within the spreadsheet itself) which host the values you want to include in the function, or define the appropriate cell range.
Works Suite 2000 inserts the cell references and the relevant operator(s) into the dialog.

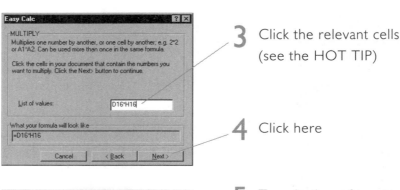

3 Click the relevant cells (see the HOT TIP)

4 Click here

Re step 5 – alternatively, click the cell within the spreadsheet itself.

5 Type in the reference of the cell where you want the function inserted

6 Click here to insert the function

Cell protection

Specific cells can be protected so that their contents are not overwritten. This is a two-stage process:

By default, all spreadsheet cells are locked, but not protected.

1. 'unlocking' those cells which you'll want to amend later (and therefore don't want to protect)

2. protecting the cells which are still locked (cell locking is ineffective until you do this)

You can also protect the active spreadsheet in its entirety.

Unlocking and protecting specific cells

Select the cells you *don't* want to protect. Pull down the Format menu and carry out steps 1, 2 and 4 below. Now (ensuring no cells are selected) pull down the Format menu again and carry out steps 1, 3 and 4 below:

1 Click here

2 Ensure Locked is deselected

Re step 3 – Works Suite 2000 protects those cells which have not been unlocked in the first stage in this operation.

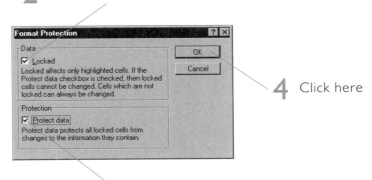

4 Click here

3 Ensure Protect Data is ticked

Protecting *all* cells in a spreadsheet

Pull down the Format menu and click Protection. Do the following:

The procedures here assume that no cells have been unlocked (see
page 113).

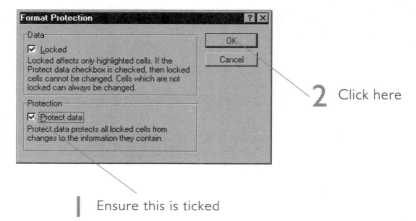

2 Click here

| Ensure this is ticked

If you want to remove cell protection, follow steps 1-2 again. (In step 1, however, ensure Protect data isn't ticked).

The effects of cell protection

When you've protected cells, the following results apply:

1. any attempt to overwrite/edit a locked cell produces a special message:

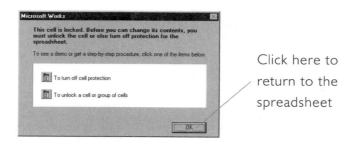

Click here to return to the spreadsheet

2. when a locked cell is selected, certain menu commands are greyed out

Amending row/column sizes

Sooner or later, you'll find it necessary to change the dimensions of rows or columns. This necessity arises when there is too much data in cells to display adequately. You can enlarge or shrink single or multiple rows/columns.

Changing row height

To change one row's height, click the row heading. If you want to change multiple rows, hold down Shift and click the appropriate extra headings. Then pull down the Format menu and click Row Height. Carry out the following steps:

2 Click here

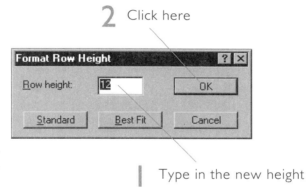

Works Suite 2000 has a useful 'best fit' feature. Simply click Best Fit in either dialog to have the row(s) or column(s) adjust themselves automatically to their contents.

Type in the new height

Changing column width

To change one column's width, click the column heading. If you want to change multiple columns, hold down Shift and click the appropriate extra headings. Then pull down the Format menu and click Column Width. Now do the following:

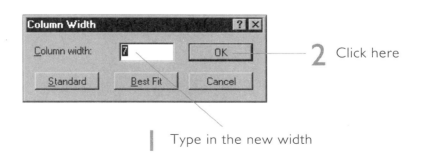

2 Click here

Type in the new width

Inserting rows or columns

You can insert additional rows or columns into spreadsheets.

Inserting a new row or column

First, select one or more cells within the row(s) or column(s) where you want to carry out the insert operation. Now pull down the Insert menu and carry out step 1 OR 2 below, as appropriate:

If you select cells in more than one row or column, Works Suite 2000 inserts the equivalent number of new rows or columns.

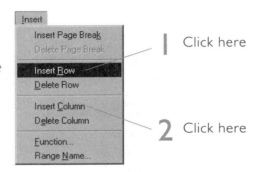

1 Click here

2 Click here

The new row(s) or column(s) are inserted immediately.

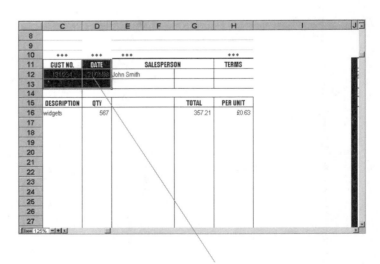

Here, two new columns or three new rows are being added

Working with fills

The Spreadsheet module lets you duplicate the contents of a selected cell down a column or across a row, easily and conveniently.

Use this technique to save time and effort.

Duplicating a cell

Click the cell whose contents you want to duplicate. Then move the mouse pointer over the appropriate border; the pointer changes to a cross and the word FILL appears:

Here, cell A3 has been selected.

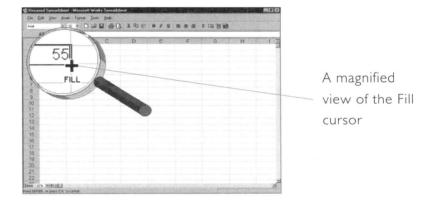

A magnified view of the Fill cursor

Click and hold down the button; drag the border over the cells into which you want the contents inserted. Release the button.

The contents of A3 have been copied to A4:A15.

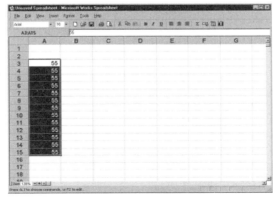

Using AutoFill

You can also carry out intelligent fills which *extrapolate* cell contents over the specified cells – Works calls these 'data series'. Look at the next illustration:

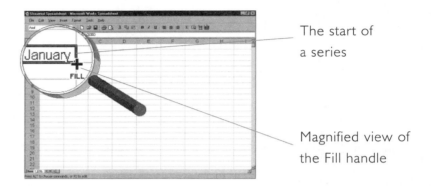

The start of a series

Magnified view of the Fill handle

If (as here) you wanted to insert month names progressively in successive cells in a column, you could do so manually. But there's a much easier way. You can use AutoFill.

Using AutoFill to create a series

Type in the first element(s) of the series in a cell or consecutive cells. Select the cell(s). Then position the mouse pointer over the Fill handle in the bottom right-hand corner of the last cell (the pointer changes to a cross-hair). Hold down the left mouse button and drag the handle over the cells into which you want to extend the series. When you release the mouse button, Works Suite 2000 extrapolates the initial entry or entries into the appropriate series.

In addition to months, data series can consist of the following:

- *numbers (e.g. 1, 2, 3, 4 etc.)*
- *days of the week*
- *years, and;*
- *alphanumeric combinations (e.g. Week 1, Week 2, Week 3 etc.)*

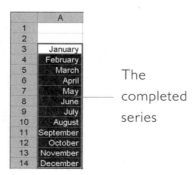

The completed series

Working with headers

To edit an existing header, simply follow the procedures outlined here; in step 1, amend the current header text as necessary.

You can have the Spreadsheet print text at the top of each page within a document; the area of the page where repeated text appears is called the 'header'. In the same way, you can have text printed at the base of each page; in this case, the relevant page area is called the 'footer'. Headers and footers are printed within the top and bottom page margins, respectively.

Inserting a header

Pull down the View menu and click Headers and Footers. Now do the following:

Type in header text

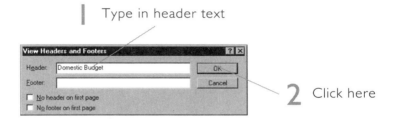

2 Click here

Viewing headers

You can only view headers in Print Preview mode.

Launch Print Preview mode – see page 140 for how to do this.

It isn't possible to amend the formatting of text in spreadsheet headers.

A header viewed in Print Preview

Working with footers

To edit an existing footer, simply follow the procedures outlined here; in step 1, amend the current footer text as necessary.

You can have the Spreadsheet automatically print text at the bottom of each page within a document; the area of the page where repeated text appears is called the 'footer'.

Footers are often used to display an abbreviated version of the spreadsheet's title.

Inserting a footer

Pull down the View menu and click Headers and Footers. Now do the following:

Type in footer text

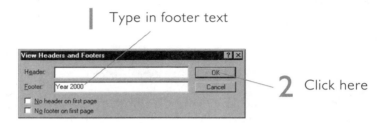

2 Click here

You can only view footers in Print Preview mode.

Viewing footers

Launch Print Preview mode – see page 140 for how to do this.

It isn't possible to amend the formatting of text in spreadsheet footers.

A footer viewed in Print Preview

Changing number formats

The Spreadsheet module lets you apply various formatting enhancements to cells and their contents. You can:

Number formats let you specify a variety of options. These include:

- specify a number format

- customise the font, type size and style of contents

- specify cell alignment

- border and/or shade cells

Fixed, Number, Percent, Currency & Exponential

You specify the no. of decimal places

Specifying a number format

You can customise the way cell contents (e.g. numbers and dates/times) display. For example, you can specify at what point numbers are rounded up. Available formats are organised under several general categories. These include: Date, Percent and Fraction.

Date & Time

You specify the format (e.g. 17 April 2000 or 02:54 PM)

Fraction

You specify how fractions are rounded up

Select the cells whose contents you want to customise. Pull down the Format menu and click Number. Now do the following:

True/False, General and Text

No options

Ensure the Number tab is active

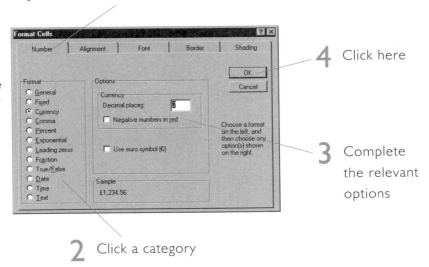

Re step 3 – the options you can choose from vary according to the category chosen.
Complete them as necessary.

4 Click here

3 Complete the relevant options

2 Click a category

Changing fonts and styles

The Spreadsheet module lets you carry out the following actions on cell contents (numbers, text or combinations of both). You can apply:

- a new font

- a new type size

- a font style (*Italic,* Bold, <u>Underlining</u> or ~~Strikethrough~~)

- a colour

Amending the appearance of cell contents

Select the cell(s) whose contents you want to reformat. Pull down the Format menu and click Font and Style. Now follow any of steps 1-4 (as appropriate) below. Finally, carry out step 5.

1 Click a font   2 Type in a type size

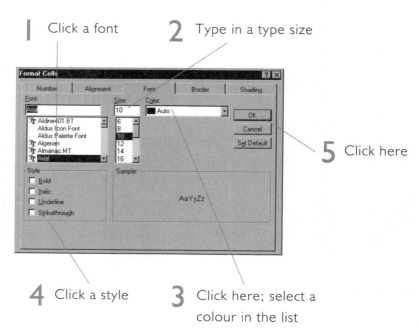

Re step 4 – you can apply multiple styles (e.g. Bold and Italic) if required.

5 Click here

4 Click a style   3 Click here; select a colour in the list

Cell alignment

By default, Works Suite 2000 aligns text to the left of cells, and numbers to the right. However, if you want you can change this.

You can specify alignment under two broad headings: Horizontal and Vertical.

Horizontal alignment

The main options are:

General	the default (see above)
Left	contents are aligned from the left
Right	contents are aligned from the right
Center	contents are centred
Fill	contents are duplicated so that they fill the cell
Center across selection	contents are centred across more than one cell (if you pre-selected a cell range)

Vertical alignment

Available options are:

Top	cell contents align with the top of the cell(s)
Center	contents are centred
Bottom	contents align with the cell bottom

Most of these settings parallel features found in Word 2000 (and in many other word processors). The difference, however, lies in the fact that in spreadsheets Works Suite 2000 has to align data within the bounds of cells rather than a page. When it aligns text, it often needs to employ its own version of text wrap. See overleaf for more information on this.

By default, when text is too large for the host cell, Works Suite 2000 overflows the surplus into adjacent cells to the right. However, you can opt to have the Spreadsheet module force the text onto separate lines within the original cell. This process is called text wrap.

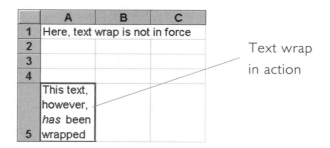

Text wrap in action

Customising cell alignment & applying text wrap

Select the relevant cell(s). Pull down the Format menu and click Alignment. Now follow any or all of steps 1-3 (as appropriate) below. Finally, carry out step 4:

3 Click a vertical alignment

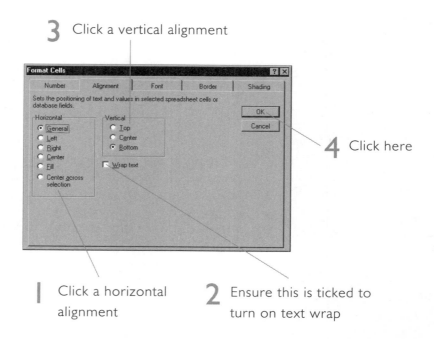

4 Click here

1 Click a horizontal alignment

2 Ensure this is ticked to turn on text wrap

Bordering cells

Bordering cells is a useful technique. Reasons you might want to do this include:

- *to emphasise cells or cell ranges, and;*
- *to create individual lines for graphical effect (especially if gridlines are turned off)*

Works Suite 2000 lets you define a border around:

- the perimeter of a selected cell range
- the individual cells within a selected cell range
- specific sides within a cell range

You can customise the border by choosing from a selection of pre-defined border styles. You can also colour the border, if required.

Applying a cell border

First, select the cell range you want to border. Pull down the Format menu and click Border. Now carry out steps 1-2 below. Step 3 is optional. Finally, follow step 4::

Re step 1 – Outline borders the perimeter of the selected cells.

The other options (you can click more than 1) affect individual sides.

| Click a border – see the HOT TIP

2 Click a line style

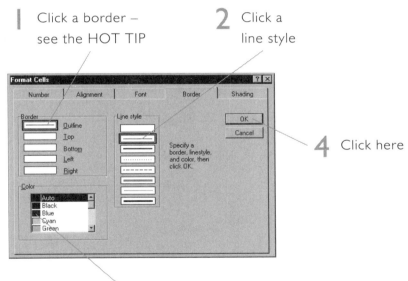

4 Click here

If you're setting multiple border options, repeat steps 1-3 as required, before you carry out step 4.

3 Click a colour

To remove a border, select the relevant cells. Launch the Format Cells dialog with the Border tab active. In the Border section, click the border you want to disable. In the Line style section, click this:

Repeat the above until all the borders have been removed. Finally, click OK.

Shading cells

Works Suite 2000 lets you apply the following to cells:

- a pattern

- a foreground colour

- a background colour

You can do any of these singly, or in combination. Interesting effects can be achieved by using foreground colours with coloured backgrounds.

Applying a pattern or background

First, select the cell range you want to shade. Pull down the Format menu and click Shading. Now follow steps 1, 2 and/ or 3 as appropriate. Finally, carry out step 4:

Click a shading or pattern

The Sample area previews how your shading will look.

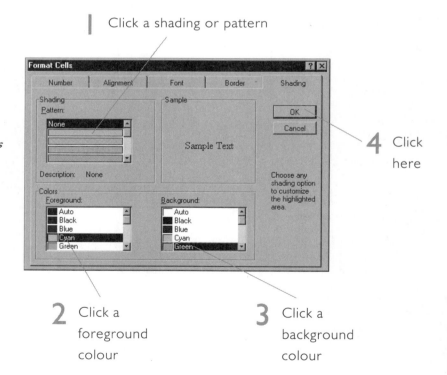

4 Click here

2 Click a foreground colour

3 Click a background colour

AutoFormat

Works Suite 2000 provides a shortcut to the formatting of spreadsheet data: AutoFormat.

You can undo (reverse) AutoFormats by pressing Ctrl+Z immediately after imposing them. (This technique also works with most other Spreadsheet editing actions.)

AutoFormat consists of 16 pre-defined formatting schemes. These incorporate specific excerpts from the font, number, alignment, border and shading options discussed earlier. You can apply any of these schemes (and their associated formatting) to selected cell ranges with just a few mouse clicks. Doing this saves a lot of time and effort, and the results are dependably professional.

AutoFormat works with most arrangements of spreadsheet data. However, if the effect you achieve isn't what you want, see the DON'T FORGET tip.

Using AutoFormat

First, select the cell range you want to apply an automatic format to. Pull down the Format menu and click AutoFormat. Now carry out steps 1 and 2 below:

2 Click here

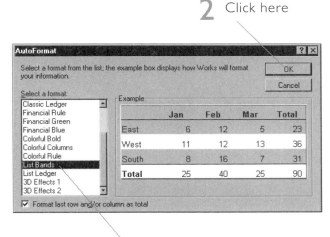

The Example field previews how your data will look with the specified AutoFormat.

Click the format you want to apply

Find operations

The Spreadsheet lets you search for and jump to text and/or numbers (in short, any information) in your spreadsheets. This is a particularly useful feature when spreadsheets become large and complex, as they almost invariably do.

In Find operations, you can specify whether Works Suite 2000 searches:

- by columns or rows

- in cells which contain formulas

- in cells which don't contain formulas

Searching for data

Place the mouse pointer at the location in the active spreadsheet from which you want the search to begin. Pull down the Edit menu and click Find. (Or press Ctrl+F.) Now carry out step 1 below, then either of steps 2-3. Finally, carry out step 4:

1 Type in the data you want to find

4 Click here

If you want to restrict the search to specific cells, select a cell range before you follow steps 1-4.

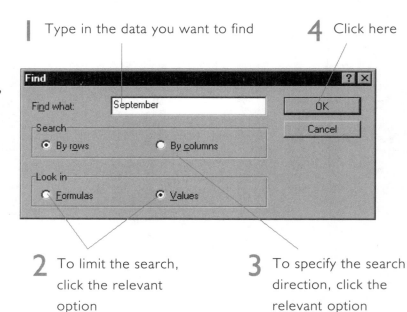

2 To limit the search, click the relevant option

3 To specify the search direction, click the relevant option

Search-and-replace operations

When you search for data, you can also – if you want – have Works Suite 2000 replace it with something else.

Search-and-replace operations can be organised by rows or by columns. However, unlike straight searches, you can't specify whether Works looks in cells which contain formulas or those which don't.

Running a search-and-replace operation

Place the mouse pointer at the location in the active spreadsheet from which you want the search to begin. Pull down the Edit menu and click Replace. Carry out steps 1-3 below. Now do *one* of the following:

— Follow step 4. When Works locates the first search target, carry out step 5 to have it replaced. Repeat this process as often as necessary

— Carry out step 6 to have Works find every target and replace it automatically

If you want to restrict the search-and-replace operation to specific cells, select a cell range before you follow the procedures outlined here.

1 Type in the search data

4 Click here to find the 1st occurrence

5 Click here to replace it

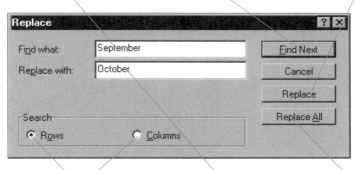

3 To specify the search direction, click the relevant option

2 Type in the replacement data

6 Click here to replace *all* occurrences

Charting – an overview

The Spreadsheet module has comprehensive charting capabilities. You can have it convert selected data into its visual equivalent. To do this, Works Suite 2000 offers 12 chart formats:

Charts make data more attractive, and therefore easier to take in.

- Area
- Bar
- Line
- Pie
- Stacked Line
- X-Y (Scatter)

- Radar
- Combination
- 3-D Area
- 3-D Bar
- 3-D Line
- 3-D Pie

Works Suite 2000 uses a special dialog to make the process of creating charts as easy and convenient as possible.

The illustration below shows a sample 3-D Area chart:

When you create a chart, Works Suite 2000 launches it in a separate Chart Editor window.
You can have as many as 8 charts associated with any spreadsheet.

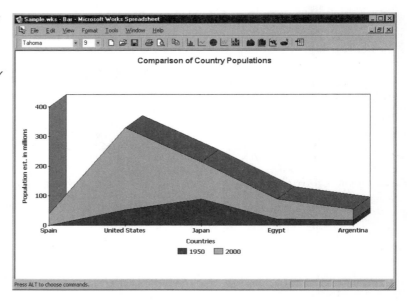

Creating a chart

When you select the data cells, include a row or column of text entries if you want these inserted into the chart as descriptive labels.

Select the cells you want to view as a chart. Pull down the Tools menu and click Create New Chart. Carry out steps 1-3 below. Follow steps 4-6 if you need to set advanced chart options. If you didn't follow steps 4-6, carry out step 7.

I Ensure the Basic Options tab is active

If this is the first time you've created a chart (or if you haven't yet performed step A below) an extra dialog launches before step 1. Do the following:

A Select this   **B** Click here

Now complete steps 1-6.

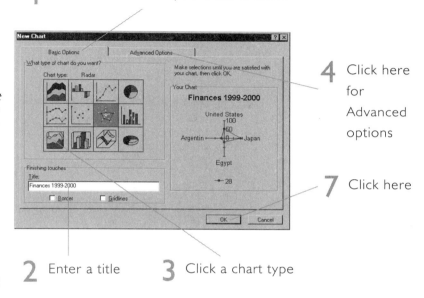

4 Click here for Advanced options

7 Click here

2 Enter a title   **3** Click a chart type

5 Complete this section, as appropriate

When you've just created a chart, you may find the effect isn't what you wanted. If so, you can fine-tune the data series it's based on.

Pull down the Edit menu and click Series. In the Edit Series dialog, amend the value and category series, as appropriate. Click OK to redraw the chart.

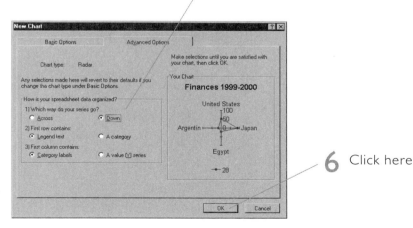

6 Click here

Amending chart formats

Once you've created a chart, you can easily change the underlying chart type. You can also apply a new sub-type.

Each basic chart type has several sub-types (variations) associated with it.

These are unavailable when you first create your chart.

Switch to the chart you want to reformat (if it isn't already open, first follow the procedure under 'Viewing charts' on page 134). Pull down the Format menu and click Chart Type. Follow steps 1-2. If you want to apply a sub-type, carry out 3-5. If you *didn't* follow steps 3-5, follow step 6.

1 Ensure the Basic Types tab is active

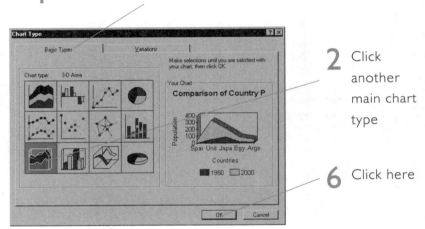

2 Click another main chart type

6 Click here

3 Click the Variations tab

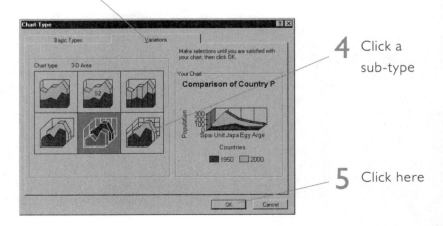

4 Click a sub-type

5 Click here

Reformatting charts

Text which is selected (like all chart objects) is surrounded by handles:

You can reformat charts in the following ways. You can:

- apply a new typeface/type size/font style to text

- apply a new colour/shade to graphic components

Reformatting text

Within the open chart, click the text you want to change. Pull down the Format menu and click Font and Style. Carry out any of steps 1-4, as appropriate. Finally, follow step 5:

The series in a chart are the individual data entries. Below are sample series from a 3D bar chart:

2 Type in a type size

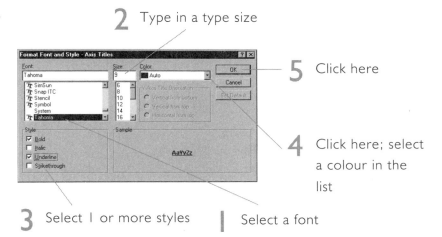

5 Click here

4 Click here; select a colour in the list

3 Select 1 or more styles

1 Select a font

Re step 3 – click Format All instead to apply the changes to all related value series.

Reformatting graphic objects

Double-click the object (e.g. a series) you want to reformat. Carry out step 1 and/or 2 below. Finally, follow step 3.

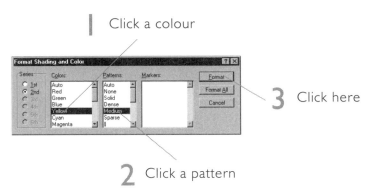

1 Click a colour

3 Click here

2 Click a pattern

To close the Format Shading and Color dialog, click this button:

after step 3.

Chart housekeeping

You can't select more than one chart at a time here. To view multiple charts, simply repeat this procedure as often as required.

Viewing charts

A Works Suite 2000 spreadsheet can have a maximum of 8 charts associated with it. To view a chart (when the spreadsheet or another chart is on-screen), pull down the View menu and click Chart. Now do the following:

When you've finished working with your chart(s), you can return to the underlying spreadsheet by pulling down the View menu and clicking Spreadsheet.

Click a chart

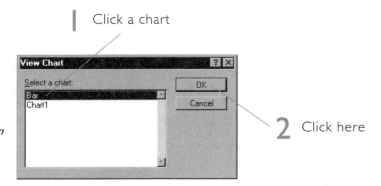

2 Click here

Deleting charts

If you want to delete more than one chart, follow steps 1-2 as often as necessary. Finally, carry out step 3.

If you try to create more than 8 charts for a particular spreadsheet, Works Suite 2000 will refuse to comply. The answer is to delete one or more unwanted charts.

Follow the procedure above to switch to the chart you want to remove. Pull down the Tools menu and click Delete Chart. Now do the following:

After step 3, the Spreadsheet module launches a warning. Do the following:

4 Click here

Click a chart

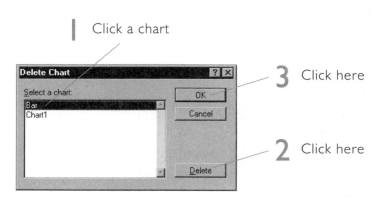

3 Click here

2 Click here

Page setup – an overview

Making sure your spreadsheets print with the correct page setup can be a complex issue, for the simple reason that most become very extensive with the passage of time (so large, in fact, that in the normal course of things they won't fit onto a single page). Luckily, Works Suite 2000 makes the entire page setup issue easy.

Page setup features you can customise include:

- the paper size

- the page orientation

- the starting page number

- margins

- whether gridlines are printed

- whether row and column headers are printed

Margin settings you can amend are:

— the top margin

— the bottom margin

— the left margin

— the right margin

Additionally, you can set the distance between the top page edge and the top of the header, and the distance between the bottom page edge and the bottom edge of the footer.

When you save your active spreadsheet, all Page Setup settings are automatically saved with it.

Setting size/orientation options

The Spreadsheet module comes with 17 pre-defined paper types which you can apply to your spreadsheets, in either portrait (top-to-bottom) or landscape (sideways on) orientation.

Portrait orientation

Landscape orientation

If none of the supplied page definitions is suitable, you can create your own.

Applying a new page size/orientation

Pull down the File menu and click Page Setup. Now carry out step 1 below, followed by steps 2-3 as appropriate. Finally, carry out step 4:

Ensure this tab is active

To create your own paper size, click Custom Size in step 2. Then type in appropriate measurements in the Height & Width fields. Finally, carry out steps 3-4.

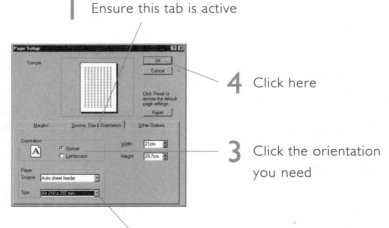

4 Click here

3 Click the orientation you need

2 Click here; click the page size you need in the drop-down list

Setting margin options

The Spreadsheet module lets you set a variety of margin settings. The illustration below shows the main ones:

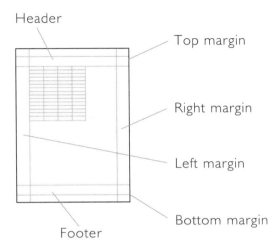

Applying new margins

Pull down the File menu and click Page Setup. Now carry out step 1 below, followed by steps 2-3 as appropriate. Finally, carry out step 4:

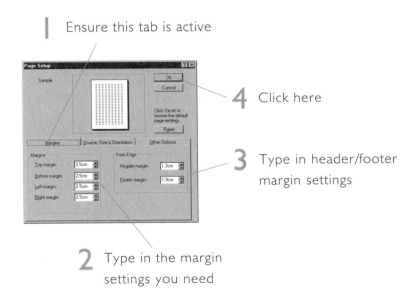

1 Ensure this tab is active

4 Click here

3 Type in header/footer margin settings

2 Type in the margin settings you need

Other page setup options

If you're unsure what column and row headings look like, refer to page 98.

(For how to view gridlines within the spreadsheet itself, see the HOT TIP on page 102.)

You can determine whether gridlines and row/column headings print.

Pull down the File menu and do the following:

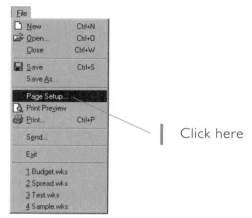

1 Click here

2 Ensure the Other Options tab is active

Re step 4 — here, you can set the page number for the first page in your spreadsheet (the default is '1').

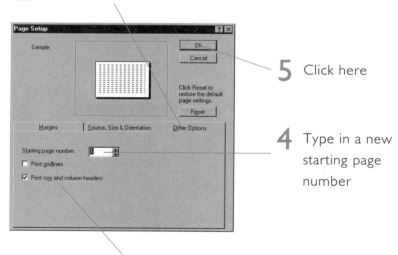

5 Click here

4 Type in a new starting page number

3 Select Print gridlines and/or Print row and column headers

Page setup for charts

Most page setup issues for charts are identical to those for spreadsheet data. However, there are differences. The following additional options are available:

Full page	the chart is expanded to fill the page, with its width/height ratio disrupted, if necessary
Full page, keep proportions	the chart is scaled to fit the page, but with its width/height ratio unaltered
Screen size	the chart is reduced to the size of your computer screen (so that it occupies roughly 25% of the page)

Customising printed chart sizes

Pull down the File menu and click Page Setup. Now carry out steps 1-3 below:

1 Ensure the Other Options tab is active

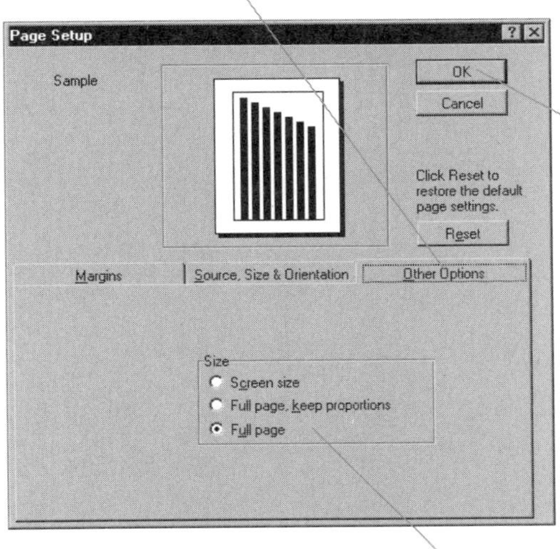

3 Click here

2 Click a scale option

Using Print Preview

If you want to preview charts, you can use an alternative route. While editing a chart, pull down the View menu and click Display as Printed. Works Suite 2000 now displays the chart in situ, as it will look when printed. You can go on editing the chart in the usual way.

(To return to the normal view, pull down the View menu and click Display as Printed again.)

The Spreadsheet module provides a special view mode called Print Preview. This displays the active spreadsheet (one page at a time) exactly as it will look when printed. Use Print Preview as a final check just before you begin printing.

When you're using Print Preview, you can zoom in or out on the active page. What you can't do, however, is:

- display more than one page at a time

- edit or revise the active spreadsheet or chart (in the case of charts, however, see the HOT TIP for a work-round)

Launching Print Preview

Pull down the File menu and click Print Preview. This is the result:

A preview of a chart

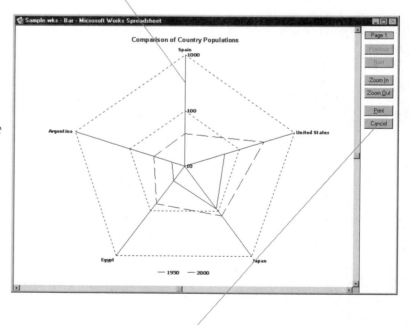

This is a Radar chart. For how to apply this and other chart types, see page 132.

You can use a keyboard shortcut to leave Print Preview mode and return to your spreadsheet or chart. Simply press Esc.

Click Cancel to leave Print Preview

Zooming in or out in Print Preview

There are two methods you can use here.

Using the mouse
Do the following:

Move the mouse pointer over the
page (it changes to a magnifying glass)

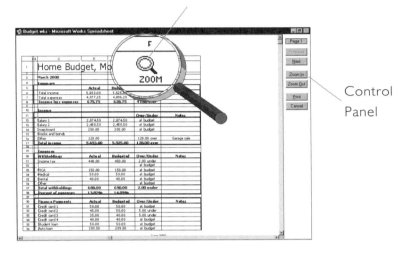

Control
Panel

*Repeat step 2
to increase the
magnification
even more.
(Doing so
again, however, returns it to
the original level.)*

2 Left-click once to increase the magnification

Using the Control Panel
Launch Print Preview. Then carry out the following actions:

*Depending on
the current
level of
magnification,
one of the
Zoom buttons may be
greyed out, and therefore
unavailable.*

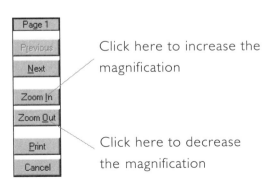

Click here to increase the
magnification

Click here to decrease
the magnification

Changing pages in Print Preview

Although you can only view one page at a time in Print Preview mode, you can step backwards and forwards through the spreadsheet as often as necessary.

There are three methods you can use (in descending order of usefulness).

Using the Control Panel

Carry out the following actions:

Depending on your location within the document (and the number of pages), one of these buttons may be greyed out, and therefore unavailable.

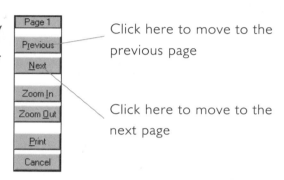

Click here to move to the previous page

Click here to move to the next page

Using the keyboard

You can use the following keyboard shortcuts:

In a magnified page view, the Page Up and Page Down keys move through the current page.

Page Up	Moves to the previous page (unavailable within a magnified page view)
Page Down	Moves to the next page (unavailable within a magnified page view)
Up cursor	Within a magnified view of a page, moves towards the top of the page
Down cursor	Within a magnified view of a page, moves towards the base of the page

Using the scrollbars

When you're working with a magnified view of a page, use the vertical and/or horizontal scrollbars (using standard Windows techniques) to move up or down within the page.

Printing spreadsheet data

When you print your data, you can specify:

- the number of copies you want printed

- whether you want the copies 'collated'. This is the process whereby Works Suite 2000 prints one full copy at a time. For instance, if you're printing five copies of a 12-page spreadsheet, Works prints pages 1-12 of the first copy, followed by pages 1-12 of the second and pages 1-12 of the third... and so on.

- which pages you want printed

- the printer you want to use (if you have more than one installed on your system)

You can 'mix and match' these, as appropriate.

Starting a print run

Open the spreadsheet containing the data you want to print. Then pull down the File menu and click Print. Perform any of steps 1-4. Then carry out step 5 to begin printing:

If you need to adjust your printer's internal settings before you initiate printing, click Properties. Then refer to your printer's manual.

If this is the first time you've printed anything (or if you haven't yet performed step A below) an extra dialog launches before step 1. Do the following:

A Select this   B Click here

Now complete steps 1-6.

Click Draft quality printing to have your spreadsheet print with minimal formatting.

1 Click here; select a printer from the list

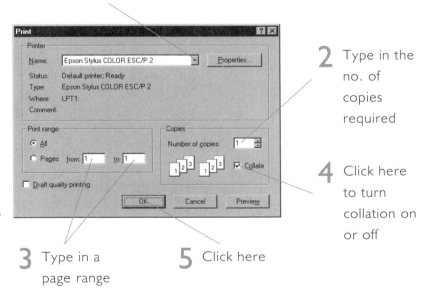

2 Type in the no. of copies required

3 Type in a page range

4 Click here to turn collation on or off

5 Click here

Printing – the fast track approach

In earlier topics, we've looked at how to customise print options to meet varying needs and spreadsheet sizes. However, the Spreadsheet module – like Word 2000 – recognises that there will be times when you won't need this level of complexity. There are occasions when you'll merely want to print out your work (often for proofing purposes):

• bypassing the Print dialog, and;

• with the current print settings applying

For this reason, Works provides a method which is much quicker and easier to use.

Printing with the default print options

First, open the spreadsheet you want to print. Ensure your printer is ready. Make sure the Toolbar is visible. (If it isn't, pull down the View menu and click Toolbar). Now do the following:

Click here

The active spreadsheet starts to print straightaway

Using HELP Contents

You can use a keyboard shortcut to launch Help: simply press F1.

Click this icon:

under the Title bar to launch Contents.

The Spreadsheet module has comprehensive HELP facilities, organised under two broad headings:

- Contents (a list of program-specific topics)

- Index (an alphabetical list of topics)

To generate the Help Contents dialog from within the Spreadsheet (or the Task Launcher), pull down the Help menu and choose Contents.

Using Contents

Do the following:

Works Suite 2000 HELP displays in a separate screen to the right of the Spreadsheet module.

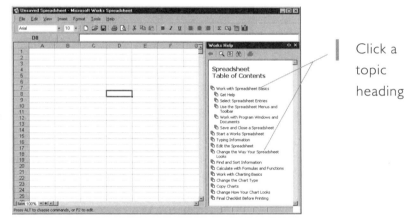

Click a topic heading

To print out HELP information, click this button immediately below the Title bar:

Complete the Print dialog, then click OK.

After step 1, Works Suite 2000 launches a series of subheadings. Click one, then select a subsidiary topic (prefixed by ⬜ instead of 🔖). Works Suite 2000 displays the topic in the HELP window.

2 When you've finished viewing the topic, click this button: ☒ in the upper right hand corner of the Contents window to close it

Using HELP Index

To generate the Help Index dialog from within the Spreadsheet module (or the Task Launcher), pull down the Help menu and choose Index.

Using Index

Do the following:

You can use a keyboard shortcut to launch Help: simply press F1.

Click this icon:

under the Title bar to launch Index.

If typing in a keyword in step 1 does not produce a relevant topic, scroll through available headings here until you locate the right one, then double-click it and omit step 2.

(If you still can't find the right heading, follow the procedures on the facing page.)

To print out HELP information, click this button immediately below the Title bar:

Complete the Print dialog, then click OK.

Type in the word you want to look up

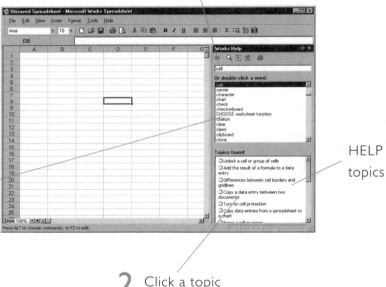

HELP topics

2 Click a topic

View the relevant topic. Finally, carry out step 3:

3 When you've finished viewing the topic, click this button: ☒ in the upper right hand corner of the Index window to close it

Using the Answer Wizard

In any HELP window, click any link (coloured green) to display further information. In the example below, the highlighted word 'scrolling' is clicked (Before); the result is a useful definition (After).

If neither of the methods on pages 145-146 works, you can use another. You can type in Plain English questions. When you've done this, you can have Works search through its HELP database for relevant topics.

Asking questions with the Answer Wizard

From any Spreadsheet HELP screen, perform steps 1-4:

Before

After

1 If the Answer Wizard isn't already displaying, click this button just below the HELP screen's Title bar:

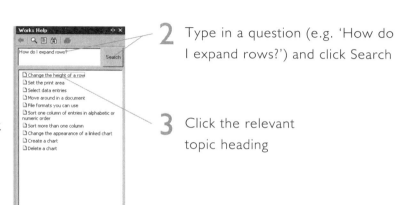

2 Type in a question (e.g. 'How do I expand rows?') and click Search

3 Click the relevant topic heading

To close the Answer Wizard, follow step 3 on the facing page.

To print out HELP information, click this button immediately below the Title bar:

Complete the Print dialog, then click OK.

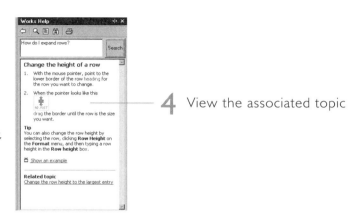

4 View the associated topic

Other ways to get assistance

There are more immediate ways to get help:

- moving the mouse pointer over Toolbar buttons produces an explanatory HELP bubble:

- Fields in dialogs have associated Help boxes. To view a box, first right-click in a field. Then carry out the following procedure:

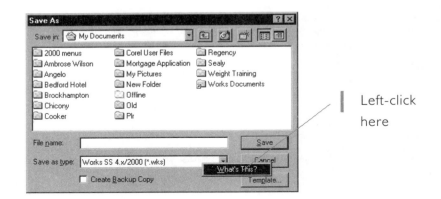

Left-click here

2 Works Suite 2000 now launches a HELP box:

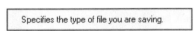

Specifies the type of file you are saving.

Other standard Windows HELP features are also present; see your Windows documentation for how to use these.

The Database

This chapter gives you the basics of using the Database. You'll learn how to work with data and formulas, and how to move around in databases (including the use of Zoom). You'll also select and locate data, and apply formatting to make it more effective. Finally, you'll generate reports, customise page layout/printing and use HELP.

Covers

Chapter Four

The Database screen

Below is a detailed illustration of a typical Database screen:

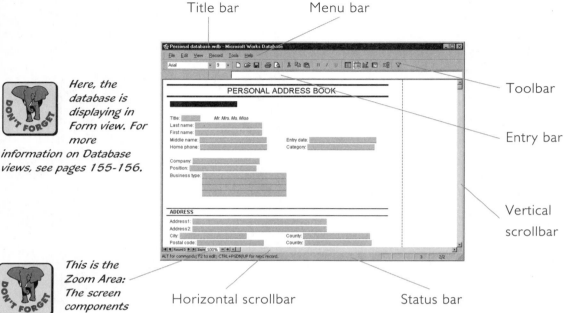

Title bar

Menu bar

Toolbar

Entry bar

Vertical scrollbar

Horizontal scrollbar

Status bar

Here, the database is displaying in Form view. For more information on Database views, see pages 155-156.

This is the Zoom Area: The screen components here are used to adjust magnification levels. See page 159.

Some of these – e.g. the rulers and scrollbars – are standard to just about all programs which run under Windows. One – the Toolbar – can be hidden, if required.

Specifying whether the Toolbar displays

Pull down the View menu and do the following:

The tick signifies that the Toolbar is currently visible.

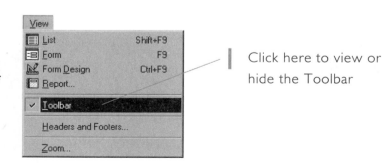

Click here to view or hide the Toolbar

Creating your first database

To start using the Task Launcher to create a new Database document, follow the procedures in the DON'T FORGET tip on page 15. Then perform steps 1-4 here.

Unlike Word 2000 and the Spreadsheet module, the Database *doesn't* create a new blank document immediately after you've launched the module from within the Task Launcher. Instead, you have to complete several dialogs first. Do the following:

Name the 1st field

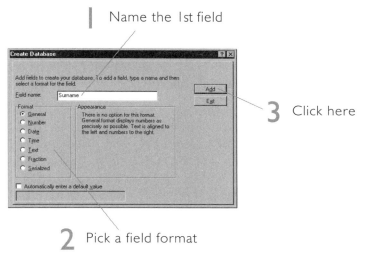

If this is the first time you've created a database (or if you haven't yet performed step A below) an extra dialog launches before step 1. Do the following:

3 Click here

2 Pick a field format

A Select this   B Click here

After you've followed step 3, Works Suite 2000 reproduces the same dialog so that you can create the second field. Repeat the above procedures as often as necessary. When you've defined your final field, do the following:

Now complete steps 1-4.

Database fields are single columns of information (in List view) or spaces for the insertion of information (in Form view).

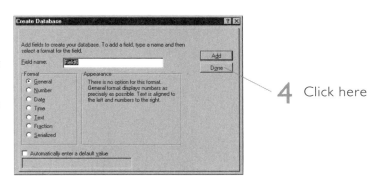

4 Click here

Entering data

When you've created a database, you can begin entering data immediately. You can enter the following basic data types:

- numbers

- text

- functions

- formulas (combinations of numbers, text and functions)

In List view, records are shown as single rows. In Form view, only one record displays on-screen at any given time.

For more information on Database views, see pages 155-156.

You enter data into 'fields'. Fields are organised into 'records'. Records are whole units of related information.

To understand this, we'll take a specific example. In an address book, the categories under which information is entered (e.g. Last name, First Name, Home Phone) are fields, while each person whose details are entered into the database constitutes one record. This is shown in the next illustration:

Fields

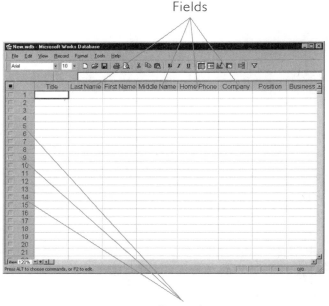

This is List view. List view is suitable for the mass insertion of data (more than 1 record is visible at a time). However, you can also enter data in Form view.

Records

You can insert the Euro symbol into databases. Fonts which support this include:

• Arial

• Courier New

• Impact

• Tahoma, and;

• Times New Roman

To insert the Euro symbol, press the Num Lock key on your keyboard. Hold down Alt and press 0128 (consecutively) on the numerical keypad. Release Alt and turn off Num Lock.

Although you can enter data *directly* into a database field (by simply clicking in it and typing it in), there's another method you can use which is often easier. Like the Database module, the Database provides a special screen component known as the Entry bar.

In the illustration below, two fields in the first record have been completed.

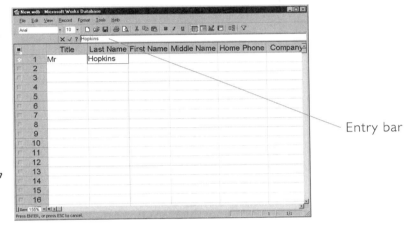

Entry bar

Here, the Zoom level has been increased to make the data more visible. For how to do this, see page 159.

Entering data via the Entry bar

Click the field you want to insert data into. Then click the Entry bar. Type in the data. Then follow step 1 below. If you decide not to proceed with the operation, follow step 2 instead:

You can use a keyboard route to confirm operations in the Entry bar. Simply press Return. (Or press Esc to cancel them.)

Click here

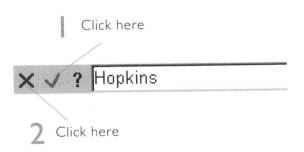

Click here

Modifying existing data

You can amend the contents of a field in two ways:

*   via the Entry bar

*   from within the field itself

When you use either of these methods, the Database enters a special state known as Edit Mode.

Amending existing data using the Entry bar

Click the field whose contents you want to change. Then click in the Entry bar. Make the appropriate revisions and/or additions. Then press Return. The relevant field is updated.

Amending existing data internally

Click the field whose contents you want to change. Press F2. Make the appropriate revisions and/or additions *within the field*. Then press Return.

The illustration below shows our new database, in Form view.

This is Form view before any formatting enhancements have been applied – for an idea of what a more developed Form view looks like, see the appropriate illustration on the facing page.

This is the first record in our database.

Using Database views

The Database module provides two principal views:

List

Pictures and most formatting components do not display in List view.

List view presents your data in a grid structure reminiscent of the Database module, with the columns denoting fields and the rows individual records.

Use List view for bulk data entry or comparison.

Form

Pictures and formatting display in Form view (although you can only initiate or modify them in Form Design view)

Form view limits the display to one record at a time, while presenting it in a way which is more visual and therefore easier on the eye. The basis of this view is the 'form', the underlying database layout which you can customise in Form Design view.

In many circumstances, Form view provides the best way to interact with your database.

Form Design view is a subset of Form view. (For how to use Form Design view, see pages 171-174).

There are two further view modes: Report (see page 181) and Print Preview (see pages 182-184).

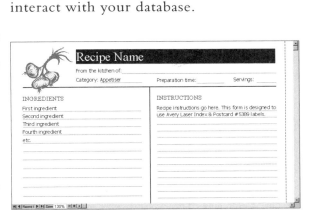

A database in Form view...

A database in List view...

...cont'd

You can use three methods to switch to another view.

The menu approach...

Pull down the View menu and do the following:

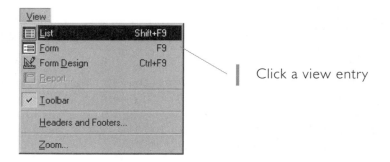

Click a view entry

If the Toolbar isn't currently on-screen, pull down the View menu and click Toolbar.

The Toolbar approach...

Refer to the Toolbar. Now click one of the following:

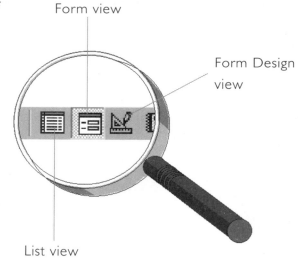

Form view

Form Design view

List view

You can also use the following keyboard shortcuts:

F9   Form view
Shift+F9   List view
Ctrl+F9   Form Design view

Moving around in databases

Databases can quickly become very large. The Database module provides several techniques you can use to find your way round.

Using the scrollbars

Use any of the following methods:

1. To scroll quickly to another record (in List view) or to another field (in Form view), drag the scroll box along the Vertical scrollbar until you reach it

2. To move one window to the right or left, click to the left or right of the scroll box in the Horizontal scrollbar

3. To move one window up or down, click above or below the scroll box in the Vertical scrollbar

4. To move up or down by one record (in List view) or one field (in Form view), click the arrows in the Vertical scrollbar

5. To move left or right by one field, click the arrows in the Horizontal scrollbar

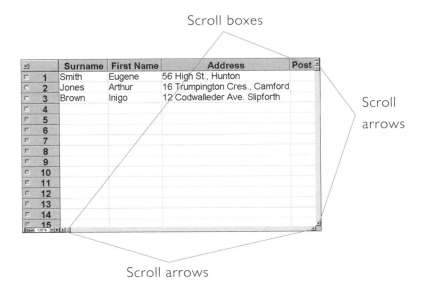

Scroll boxes

Scroll arrows

Scroll arrows

Using the keyboard

You can use the following techniques:

1. In List view, use the cursor keys to move one field left, right, up or down. In Form or Form Design views, use the up and left cursor keys to move one field up, or the down and right keys to move one field down

2. Press Home to jump to the first field in the active record, or End to move to the last

3. Press Ctrl+Home to move to the first record in the open database, or Ctrl+End to move to the last

4. Press Page Up or Page Down to move up or down by one screen

5. In Form or Form Design views, press Ctrl+Page Down to move to the next record, or Ctrl+Page Up to move to the previous one

Using the Go To dialog

You can use a keyboard shortcut to launch the Go To dialog. Simply press F5, or Ctrl+G.

The Database provides a special dialog which you can use to specify precise field or record destinations.

In any view, pull down the Edit menu and click Go To. Now carry out step 1 OR 2 below. Finally, follow step 3.

2 Type in a record number

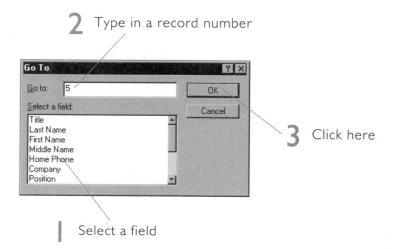

3 Click here

Select a field

Using Zoom

The ability to vary the level of magnification in the Database module is very useful. Sometimes, it's helpful to 'zoom out' (i.e. decrease the magnification) so that you can take an overview; at other times, you'll need to 'zoom in' (increase the magnification) to work in greater detail. Works Suite 2000 makes this process easy and convenient.

You can change magnification levels in the Database module:

*   with the use of the Zoom Area

*   with the Zoom dialog

Using the Zoom Area

You can use the Zoom Area (at the base of the screen) to alter zoom levels with the minimum of effort. Carry out step 1 or 2, or steps 3-4, as appropriate:

See the screen illustration on page 150 for more information on where to find the Zoom Area.

Re step 4 – clicking Custom produces the Zoom dialog (you can also launch this by selecting Zoom in the View menu).

In the dialog, do one of the following:

*   *select a preset Zoom level (e.g. 75% or 200%), or;*

*   *enter your own Zoom level in the Custom field (in the range 40-1000%)*

Finally, click OK.

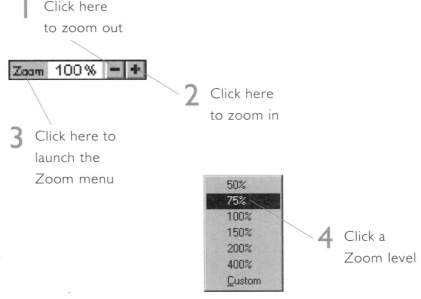

Click here to zoom out

2 Click here to zoom in

3 Click here to launch the Zoom menu

4 Click a Zoom level

Selection techniques in List view

Before you can carry out any editing operations on fields or records in the Database module, you have to select them first. The available selection techniques vary according to whether you're currently using List, Form or Form Design view.

In List view, follow any of the techniques below:

Using the mouse

To select a single field	Simply click in it
To select multiple fields	Click the field in the top left-hand corner; hold down the mouse button and drag over the fields you want to highlight. Release the mouse button
To select one record	Click the record number
To select several records	Hold down Shift as you click the record numbers

With the exception of the first, selected fields are filled with black.

To select the whole of the active database in List view, press Ctrl+Shift+F8.

☑		Surname	First Name	Address	Post Code	Phone No.
☐	1	Smith	Eugene	56 High St., Hunton		
☐	2	Jones	Arthur	16 Trumping	Camford	
☐	3	Brown	Inigo	12 Codwalleder Ave.	Slipforth	

Record numbers

Pressing F8 makes the Database enter Selection Mode. When it does, the following displays in the Status bar:

EXT

Selection Mode is in force

Using the keyboard

To select multiple fields	Position the insertion point in the first field. Press F8. Use the cursor keys to extend the selection area. Press F8 when you've finished
To select a whole record	Position the insertion point in the record. Press Ctrl+F8
To select a whole field	Position the insertion point in the field. Press Shift+F8

Selection techniques in forms

Note that some of the techniques discussed here (they're clearly marked) will only work in Form Design view.

These arrow buttons can be found in the bottom left-hand corner of the Form and Form Design view screens.

Using the mouse

To select a single field	Simply click in it.
To select multiple fields	Hold down Ctrl as you click in successive fields (you must be in Form Design view to do this).
To select one record	Click any of the following:

To previous record   To final record

To first record   To next record

To select multiple field names or inserted pictures	In Form Design view, hold down Ctrl as you click successive objects.

You can insert clip art into databases, but only in Form Design view:

Ensure no item is selected. Pull down the Insert menu and click Clip Art. Use the Clip Gallery to locate and insert an image (for help with this, see page 71).

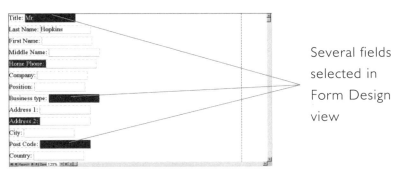

Several fields selected in Form Design view

Using the keyboard

To select a field	Use the cursor keys to position the insertion point in the relevant field
To select a record	Press Ctrl+Page Up or Ctrl+Page Down until the record you want is displayed

Formulas – an overview

You can insert formulas into Database fields. Formulas in the Database module work in much the same way as in the Spreadsheet. However, there are fewer applications for them.

Database formulas serve two principal functions:

• to ensure that the same entry appears in a given field throughout every record in a database

• to return a value based on the contents of multiple additional fields

The formula/ function appears in the Entry bar:

For the NOW() function to return a date as its result, the host field must have had the Date number format applied to it – see page 166.

Look at the next illustration:

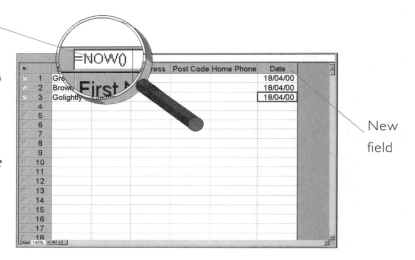

New field

Here, an extra field has been added (see page 166 for how to do this) and a formula (in this case, consisting entirely of a function) inserted. The function:

=NOW()

inserts the current system date in the Date field within every record.

Inserting a formula

As in the Spreadsheet module, all Database formulas must begin with an equals sign. This is usually followed by a permutation of the following:

Arguments (e.g. field references) relating to functions are always contained in brackets.

- one or more operands (in the case of the Database module, field names)

- a function (e.g. AVG – returns the Average)

- an arithmetical operator (+, –, /, * and ^)

The Database supports a very wide assortment of functions. For how to insert functions, refer to pages 164-165.

The arithmetical operators are (in the order in which they appear in the bulleted list above):

plus, minus, divide, multiply and *exponential*.

There are two ways to enter formulas:

Entering a formula directly into the field

Click the field into which you want to insert a formula. Then type =, followed by your formula. When you've finished defining the formula, press Return.

The Entry bar method is usually the most convenient.

Entering a formula into the Entry bar

Click the field in which you want to insert a formula. Then click in the Entry bar. Type =, followed by your formula. When you've finished defining the formula, press Return or:

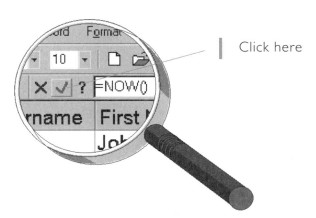

Click here

Database functions

In many ways, the Database module's implementation of functions parallels that of the Database module. However, there is one important difference: you can't use Easy Calc to insert them. Instead, you have to do so manually. Luckily, though, the inbuilt HELP system provides assistance.

For more detailed information on how to use HELP, see pages 187-189.

Using HELP before you insert a function

Pull down the Help menu and click Contents. Now do the following:

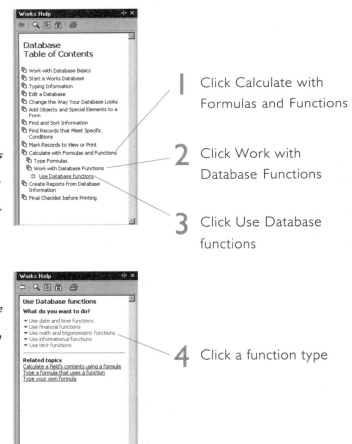

1 Click Calculate with Formulas and Functions

2 Click Work with Database Functions

3 Click Use Database functions

After step 4, click a specific function. Works Suite 2000 now launches a dedicated HELP window which tells you how to apply the relevant function:

HELP with the Date function

4 Click a function type

To close the HELP window, click this button:

in the top right-hand corner.

Inserting a function

There are two ways to insert functions:

Entering a function directly into the field

1 Click the field into which you want to insert the function

2 Type = followed by the function itself – e.g. =NOW()

3 Don't forget to include any arguments – see the tip

4 Press Enter

Re step 3 – as an example, if you're entering the AVG function (which returns the average of selected fields), type in the field details (arguments) e.g. to average fields called Week1 and Week2, type:

=AVG(Week1,Week2)

Entering a function into the Entry bar

1 Click the field into which you want to insert the function

2 Click in the Entry bar; type = followed by the function itself

3 Don't forget to include any arguments – see the tip

4 Click here

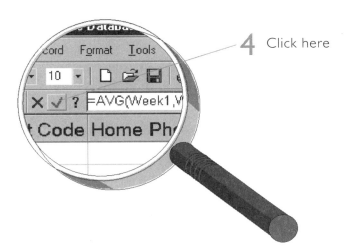

Inserting fields

You can add one or more blank fields to the active database, from Form Design (but not Form) or List view.

Adding a field in Form Design view

If you're not already in Form Design view, pull down the View menu and click Form Design. Click where you want the new field inserted. Pull down the Insert menu and click Field. Do the following:

Re step 2 – most of the number formats you can choose from are identical to those used in the Spreadsheet (see page 121 – especially the HOT TIP – for more information).

Name the new field

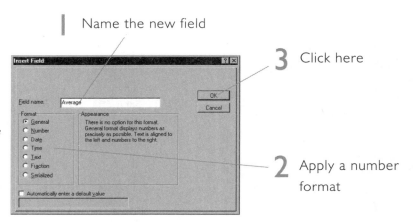

3 Click here

2 Apply a number format

Adding one or more fields in List view

If you're not currently in List view, pull down the View menu and click List. Click in the field (column) next to which you want the new field(s) added. Pull down the Record menu and click Insert Field. In the sub-menu, click Before or After, as appropriate.

The Insert Field dialog launches. Follow steps 1-2 above, then click the Add button. The dialog now changes. Do *either* of the following:

Repeat B. as often as necessary to add as many additional fields as required.

A. click Done to add the single field and close the dialog, or;

B. carry out steps 1-2 again (then click Add) to add a further field

If you carried out B., click Done when you've added the correct number of new fields.

Inserting records

You can add one or more blank records to the active database, from within either Form (but not Form Design) or List view.

See pages 157-158 for how to jump to the relevant record.

Adding a record in Form view

If you're not already in Form view, pull down the View menu and click Form. Go to the record before which you want the new record to appear. Pull down the Record menu and click Insert Record.

Adding a record in List view

If you're not currently in List view, pull down the View menu and click List. Click in the record above which you want the new record added. Pull down the Record menu and click Insert Record.

If you select more than one existing record in List view (by holding down Shift as you click the relevant row headings), Works Suite 2000 inserts the equivalent number of new records.

To hide one record in Form view, go to it. In List view, however, select one or more records. Now in either case pull down the Record menu and click Hide Record.

To make all records visible again, pull down the Record menu and click Show All Records.

Preparing to add two new records in List view...

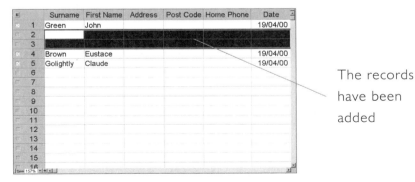

The records have been added

Amending record/field sizes

In Form or List view, you can sort database data alphanumerically.

Pull down the Record menu and click Sort Records. If the First-time Help dialog appears, (optionally) select Don't display this message in the future. Click OK. In the Sort Records dialog, click the arrow to the right of the Sort by field and select the field you want to sort by. Click Ascending or Descending.

(If you also want to sort by subsidiary fields, complete the above procedures for either – or both – Then by fields.)

Finally, click OK.

Sooner or later, you'll find it necessary to change the dimensions of fields or records within List view. This necessity arises when there is too much data to display adequately. You can enlarge or shrink single or multiple fields/records.

Changing record height

To change one record's height, click the record number. If you want to change multiple records, hold down Shift and click the appropriate extra numbers. Then pull down the Format menu and click Record Height. Carry out the following steps:

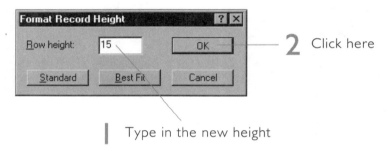

2 Click here

Type in the new height

Changing field widths

Works Suite 2000 has a useful 'best fit' feature. Simply click Best Fit in either dialog to have the record(s) or field(s) adjust themselves automatically to their contents.

(You can also achieve this by double-clicking the relevant column or row heading in List view.)

To change one field's width, click the field heading. If you want to change multiple fields, hold down Shift and click the appropriate extra headings. Then pull down the Format menu and click Field Width. Now do the following:

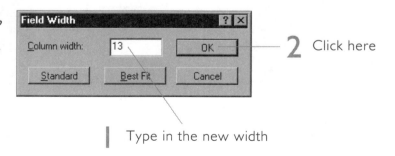

2 Click here

Type in the new width

Working with fills

You can 'filter' your data. Filters are criteria which determine which data is viewed. (For example, in an address book you could specify that only records whose Initials are 'S.' should display...)

To create and apply a filter, pull down the Tools menu and click Filters. If the First-time Help dialog appears, (optionally) select Don't display this message in the future. Click OK. In the Filter Name dialog, name the filter and click OK. Click the arrow to the right of the Field name box; select a field. Click the arrow to the right of the Comparison field; select a comparison type. In the Compare To field, type the text or values you want Works Suite 2000 to match. Repeat the above – if applicable – for additional fields below the first (remembering to select AND or OR in the box to the left) as a way of further refining the filter.

Finally, click Apply Filter.

In List view, you can have the contents of a selected field entry automatically copied into other field entries or records.

Use this technique to save time and effort.

Duplicating a field entry

Click the field entry whose contents you want to duplicate. Then move the mouse pointer over the appropriate border. Click and hold down the button; drag the border over the field entries or records into which you want the contents inserted. Release the button.

Here, the contents of the Home Phone field in record I will be copied into the same field in records 2-3

Now pull down the Edit menu and click Fill Right or Fill Down, as appropriate.

To remove the effects of applying a filter, pull down the Record menu and click Show, All Records.

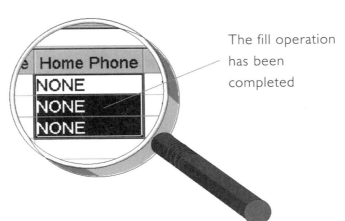

The fill operation has been completed

Working with fill series

You can spell-check database contents. Press F7. Complete the Spelling dialog in line with steps 1-4 on page 67 (ignore the references to grammar-checking).

You can also carry out fills which *extrapolate* field entry contents over the specified entries. Look at the next illustration:

The start of a series

Re step 2 —the step value sets the rate by which the series progresses. Use plus numbers for increments, minus numbers for decrements.

For example, setting '-2' in this instance would produce the following series:

• *November, September, July, May, March, January (and so on...)*

whereas '3' would give:

• *April, July, October, January (and so on...)*

If (as here) you wanted to insert progressive month names in successive field entries, you could do so manually. But there's a much easier way. You can have Works do it for you.

Creating a series

Type in the first element(s) of the series in 1 or more consecutive fields. Select all the fields (including those into which you want the series extended). Pull down the Edit menu and click Fill Series. Now do the following:

This is the result of applying the series on the right:

The completed series

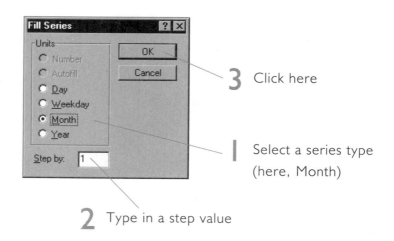

3 Click here

| Select a series type (here, Month)

2 Type in a step value

Changing fonts and styles

You can apply any of these formatting enhancements from within List or Form Design views. Note, however, that the results are independent – e.g. you can colour the same field red in Form Design view and blue in List view.

The Database module lets you carry out the following actions on field contents (numbers, text or combinations of both). You can:

• apply a new font

• apply a new type size

• apply a font style (*Italic,* Bold, <u>Underlining</u> or ~~Strikethrough~~)

• apply a colour

Amending the appearance of field contents

Select the data you want to reformat. Pull down the Format menu and click Font and Style. Now follow any of steps 1-4, as appropriate. Finally, carry out step 5.

1 Select a font

2 Type in a type size

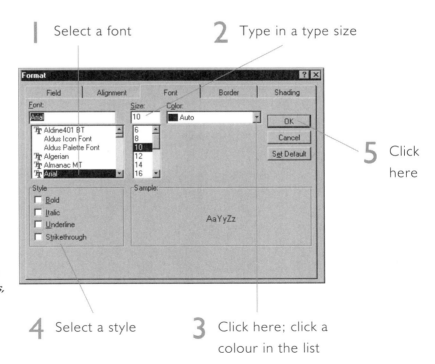

5 Click here

Re step 4 – you can apply multiple styles, if you want.

4 Select a style

3 Click here; click a colour in the list

Aligning field contents

You can apply the following alignments to field entries:

Horizontal alignment

General	the default (text to the left, numbers to the right)
Left	contents are aligned from the left
Right	contents are aligned from the right
Center	contents are centred

Vertical alignment

Top	contents align with the top of the field(s)
Center	contents are centred
Bottom	contents align with the base of the field(s)

Customising alignment & applying text wrap

Select the relevant field(s). Pull down the Format menu and click Alignment. Now follow any or all of steps 1-3, as appropriate. Finally, carry out step 4.

You can carry out any of these from within List or Form Design views. Note, however, that the full alignment options are only available within List view.

This is the List view version of the dialog.

Re step 3 – select Wrap text in List view to have any surplus text within a field forced onto separate lines within the field.

(Alternatively, in Form Design view select Slide to left to have Works Suite 2000 change the field height to accommodate text.)

Select a horizontal alignment

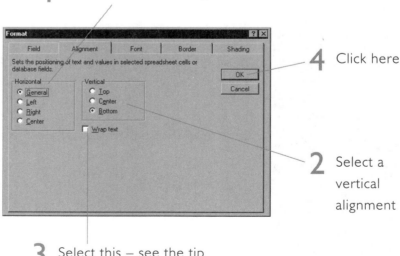

4 Click here

2 Select a vertical alignment

3 Select this – see the tip

Bordering fields

You can border fields in Form Design view, too. However, you can only create perimeter borders.

In List view, you can define a border around:

- the perimeter of selected field(s)

- the individual fields *within* a group of selected fields

- specific field sides

You can customise the border by choosing from a selection of pre-defined border styles. You can also colour it, if required.

Applying a field border

First, click the heading(s) of the field(s) you want to border. Pull down the Format menu and click Border. Now carry out steps 1 and 2 below. Step 3 is optional. (If you're setting multiple border options, repeat steps 1-3 as required). Finally, carry out step 4:

Re step 1 – Outline (unavailable in List view) borders the perimeter of the selected field(s). The other options (you can click more than 1) are only available in Form Design view and affect individual sides.

Select the extent of the border (see the HOT TIP)

4 Click here

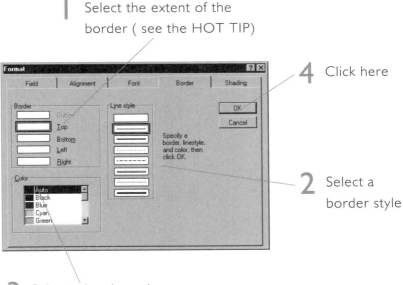

2 Select a border style

3 Select a border colour

Shading fields

In List view, you can apply the following to fields:

- a pattern

- a foreground colour

- a background colour

You can apply these effects in Form Design view, too. Note, however, that if no fields have been pre-selected they apply to the whole of the form (and the dialog below is slightly different).

You can do any of these singly, or in combination. Interesting effects can be achieved by using foreground colours with coloured backgrounds.

Applying a pattern or background

First, select the heading(s) of the field(s) you want to shade. Pull down the Format menu and click Shading. Now carry out step 1 below. Follow step 2 and/or 3 as appropriate. Finally, carry out step 4:

| Select a shading or pattern

The Sample field previews how your shading will look.

Format

| Field | Alignment | Font | Border | Shading |

Shading
Pattern:
None

Description: None

Sample

Sample Text

OK
Cancel

Choose any shading option to customize the highlighted area.

Colors
Foreground:
Auto
Black
Blue
Cyan
Green

Background:
Auto
Black
Blue
Cyan
Green

4 Click here

2 Click here; select a foreground colour

3 Click here; select a background colour

Find operations

The Database module lets you search for text and/or numbers. There are two basic options. You can:

- have the first matching record display

- view all records which contain the specified text or numbers

You can only carry out find operations in List or Form views.

Searching for data

Pull down the Edit menu and click Find. Now carry out step 1 below, then *either* step 2 or 3. Finally, carry out step 4:

You can also use a keyboard shortcut to launch the Find dialog. Simply press Ctrl+F.

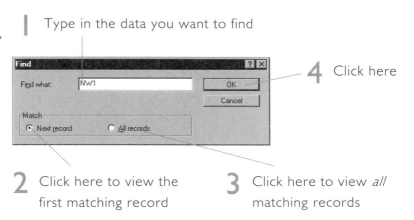

1 Type in the data you want to find

4 Click here

2 Click here to view the first matching record

3 Click here to view *all* matching records

If the Find dialog does not allow you to carry out a precise enough search, use filters instead. (See the DON'T FORGET tip on page 169 for how to use them).

Showing all records again

If you followed step 3 above, Works Suite 2000 will only display matching records (other records in your database are inaccessible). To show all records again, pull down the Record menu and do the following:

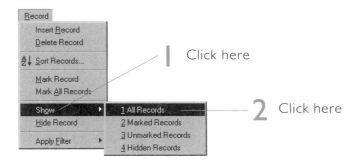

1 Click here

2 Click here

Search-and-replace operations

When you search for data, you can also – if you want – have Works Suite 2000 replace it with something else.

You can specify the following search directions:

Records   the search is left-to-right

Fields   the search is top-to-bottom

Running a search-and-replace operation

Pull down the Edit menu and click Replace. Carry out steps 1-3 below. Now do *one* of the following:

— Follow step 4. When Works locates the first search target, carry out step 5 to have it replaced. Repeat this process as often as necessary.

— Carry out step 6 to have Works find *every* target and replace it automatically.

You can only carry out search-and-replace operations in List view.

You can also use a keyboard shortcut to launch the Replace dialog. Simply press Ctrl+H.

| Type in the data you want to find

4 Click here to find the 1st occurrence

5 Click here

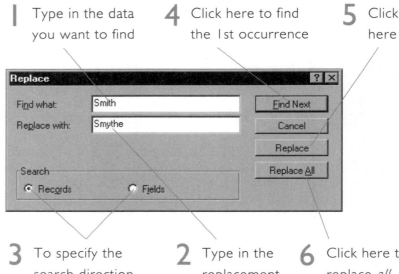

3 To specify the search direction, click the relevant option

2 Type in the replacement data

6 Click here to replace *all* occurrences

Page setup – an overview

When you come to print out your database, it's important to ensure the page setup is correct. Luckily, Works makes this easy.

See the HOT TIP on page 180 for extra page setup features which are only available in Form and Form Design views.

Page setup features you can customise (in List and Form views) include:

- the paper size

- the page orientation

- the starting page number

- margins

- whether gridlines are printed

- whether record and field headings are printed

Field headings

This is a section of a database viewed in Print Preview mode – see pages

182-184.

	Surname	First Name	Address	Post Code	Phone No.
1	Smith	Eugene	56 High St., Hunton		
2	Jones	Arthur	16 Trumping Camford		
3	Brown	Inigo	12 Codwalleder Ave. Slipforth		
4	Smith				

Record headings

Margin settings you can amend are:

— the top margin

— the bottom margin

— the left margin

— the right margin

When you save your active database, all page setup settings are saved with it.

Setting size/orientation options

The Database module comes with 17 pre-defined paper types which you can apply to your databases, in either portrait (top-to-bottom) or landscape (sideways on) orientation.

Portrait orientation

Landscape orientation

If none of the supplied page definitions is suitable, you can create your own.

Applying a new page size/orientation

Pull down the File menu and click Page Setup. Now carry out step 1 below, followed by steps 2-3 as appropriate. Finally, carry out step 4:

Ensure this tab is active

To create your own paper size, click Custom Size in step 2. Then type in the relevant measurements in the Height & Width fields. Finally, carry out steps 3-4.

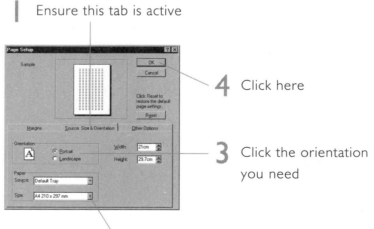

4 Click here

3 Click the orientation you need

2 Click here; click the page size you need in the drop-down list

Setting margin options

The Database module lets you set a variety of margin settings. The illustration below shows the main ones:

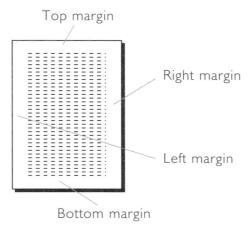

Applying new margins

Pull down the File menu and click Page Setup. Now carry out step 1-3 below:

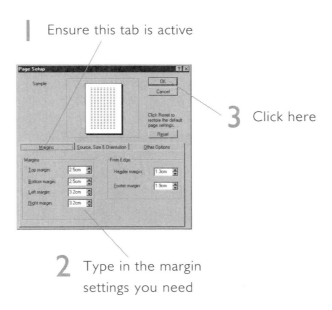

Other page setup options

You can determine whether gridlines and record/field headers print. These are demonstrated below:

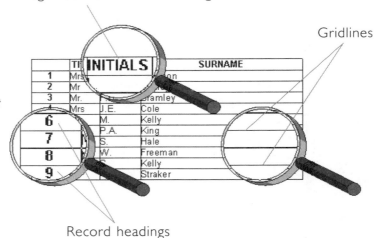

Magnified view of field heading

Gridlines

Record headings

You can also set the page number for the first page in your database – the default is '1'.
To apply a new start number, type it into the Starting page number: field.

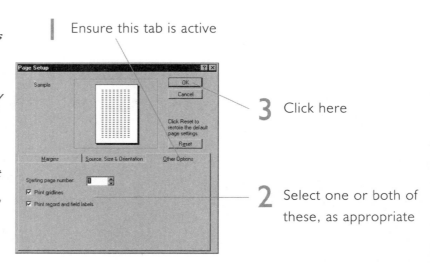

Re step 2 – if you launch this dialog from within Form or Form Design view, you can select the following instead:

Print field lines	*enables lines between fields*
Page breaks between records	*records are separated by page breaks*
All items	*all fields print*
Field entries only	*only field entries print*

You can also specify a gap between records (by entering it in the Space between records field).

Printing gridlines and record/field headings

Pull down the File menu and click Page Setup. Now carry out step 1 below, followed by step 2 as appropriate. Finally, carry out step 3:

Ensure this tab is active

3 Click here

2 Select one or both of these, as appropriate

Report creation

Reports organise – and allow you to view – database information.

You can use a special Database feature – ReportCreator – to compile a report according to the criteria you set. When you use ReportCreator, you can specify:

- how the report is named (you can also allocate a working title/heading)

- which fields are included

- the order in which fields are arranged ('sorting')

- which records are included ('filtering')

If this is the first time you've created a report (or if you haven't yet performed step A below) an extra dialog launches before step 1. Do the following:

When a report has been generated, Works stores it in a special view mode called Report Definition. This resembles List view (but has labelled rows, not numbered records).

Creating a report

Pull down the Tools menu and click ReportCreator. Do the following:

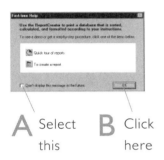

A Select this   B Click here

Now complete steps 1-4.

1 Name the report

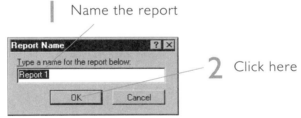

2 Click here

After step 4, click each successive dialog tab and complete the associated fields.
Finally, click Done. In this dialog:

click Preview to view the finished report in Print Preview.

3 Type in a heading   Tabs

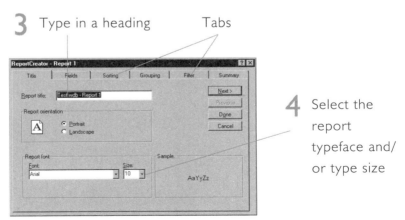

4 Select the report typeface and/ or type size

Using Print Preview

To view an existing report in Print Preview, pull down the View menu and click Report. In the View Report dialog, double-click a report.

The Database module provides a special view mode called Print Preview. This displays the active database (one page at a time) exactly as it will look when printed. Use Print Preview as a final check just before you begin printing.

When you're using Print Preview, you can zoom in or out on the active page. What you can't do, however, is:

- display more than one page at a time

- edit or revise the active document

Launching Print Preview

Pull down the File menu and click Print Preview. This is the result:

You can use a keyboard shortcut to leave Print Preview mode and return to your database. Simply press Esc.

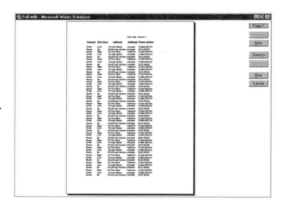

A database in List view, viewed in Print Preview

Here, the Zoom level has been increased – see the facing page.

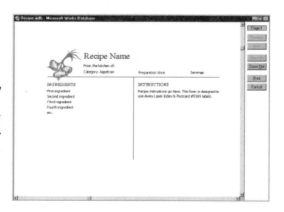

A database in Form view, viewed in Print Preview

Zooming in or out in Print Preview

There are two methods you can use here.

Using the mouse
Do the following:

Move the mouse pointer over the page (it changes to a magnifying glass)

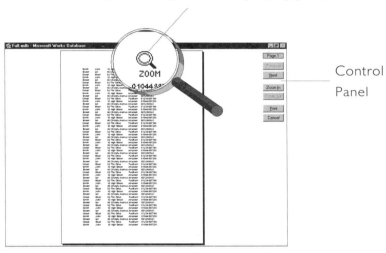

Control Panel

Repeat step 2 to increase the magnification even more. (Doing so again, however, returns it to the original level.)

2 Left-click once to increase the magnification

Using the Control Panel
Launch Print Preview. Then do one of the following:

Depending on the current level of magnification, one of the Zoom buttons may be greyed out, and therefore unavailable.

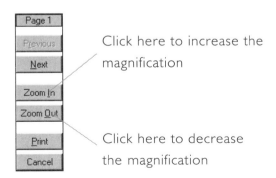

Click here to increase the magnification

Click here to decrease the magnification

Changing pages in Print Preview

Although you can only view one page at a time in Print Preview mode, you can step backwards and forwards through the database as often as necessary.

There are three methods you can use :

Using the Control Panel
Carry out the following actions:

 Depending on your location within the document (and the number of pages), one of these buttons may be greyed out, and therefore unavailable.

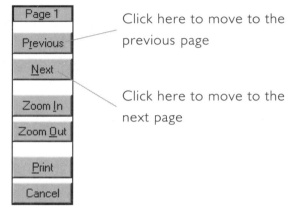

Click here to move to the previous page

Click here to move to the next page

Using the keyboard
You can use the following keyboard shortcuts:

 In a magnified page view, the Page Up and Page Down keys move through the current page.

Page Up	Moves to the previous page (but not within a magnified page view – see the HOT TIP)
Page Down	Moves to the next page (but not within a magnified page view – see the HOT TIP)
Up cursor	Within a magnified view of a page, moves towards the top of the page
Down cursor	Within a magnified view of a page, moves towards the base of the page

Using the scrollbars
When you're working with a magnified view of a page, use the vertical and/or horizontal scrollbars (using standard Windows techniques) to move up or down within the page.

Printing database data

When you print your data within List view, you can specify:

To print with the current Print dialog settings, ignore the procedures on pages 185-186. Instead, click this button in the Toolbar:

Printing begins at once.

- the number of copies you want printed

- whether you want the copies 'collated'. This is the process whereby Works Suite 2000 prints one full copy at a time. For instance, if you're printing four copies of a 20-page database, Works prints pages 1-20 of the first copy, followed by pages 1-20 of the second and pages 1-20 of the third... And so on.

- which pages you want printed

- the printer you want to use (if you have more than one installed on your system)

You can 'mix and match' these, as appropriate.

Starting a print run

Open the database which contains the data you want to print. Pull down the File menu and click Print.

If this is the first time you've initiated a print-run in your current Works Suite 2000 session, carry out steps 1-2 below, as appropriate (see the two HOT TIPS):

Re step 1 – if you click Quick tour of printing (for a guided tour explaining printing basics), follow the procedures in the two HOT TIPS on page 186. Then perform step 2 on the right, and steps 3-7 on page 186.

If, on the other hand, you select To print your document OR To print a specific page or range of pages in step 1, omit step 2 and simply carry out steps 3-7...

If you don't want to launch the printing guided tour or printing-specific assistance, omit step 1. Simply perform step 2, then steps 3-7 on page 186.

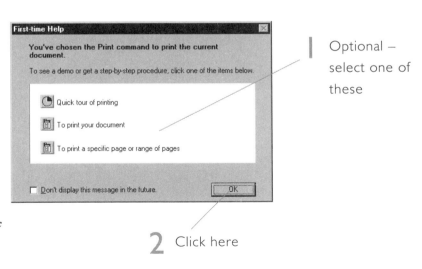

Optional – select one of these

2 Click here

...cont'd

To move through the tour, click either of these buttons:

 one screen back

 one screen on

To close the special tour at any time, click this button:

Done

If you launched the tour, follow the procedure in the HOT TIP above to close it before performing steps 2-7 on pages 185-186.

If you're printing from within Form view, you have a further choice. Click Current record only to limit the print run to the active record.

Click Draft quality printing to have your database print with minimal formatting.

If you followed step 1 on page 185, one of the following launches:

- a special tour relating to printing

- the Print dialog (plus on-screen help relating to printing)

- the Print dialog (plus help with printing page ranges)

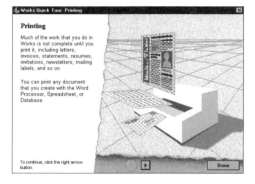

The first screen in the printing guided tour

Follow steps 3-7 below, as appropriate:

3 Click here; select a printer from the list

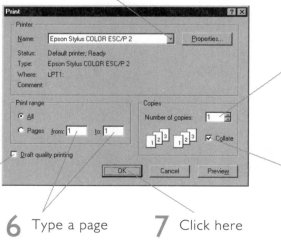

4 Type in the no. of copies required

5 Click here to turn collation on or off

6 Type a page range

7 Click here

Using HELP Contents

The Database module has comprehensive HELP facilities, organised under two broad headings:

Click this icon:

under the Title bar to launch Contents.

- Contents (a list of program-specific topics)

- Index (an alphabetical list of topics)

To generate the Help Contents dialog from within the Database (or the Task Launcher), pull down the Help menu and choose Contents.

Using Contents

Do the following:

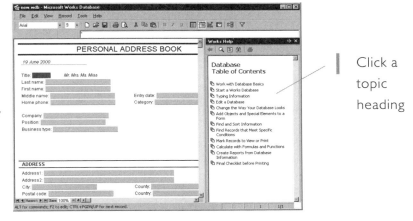

Click a topic heading

immediately below the Title bar:

Complete the Print dialog, then click OK.

After step 1, Works Suite 2000 launches a series of subheadings. Click one, then select a subsidiary topic (prefixed by ☐ instead of ▥). Works Suite 2000 displays the topic in the HELP window.

2 When you've finished viewing the topic, click this button: ✖ in the upper right hand corner of the Contents window to close it

Using HELP Index

To generate the Help Index dialog from within the Database module (or the Task Launcher), pull down the Help menu and choose Index.

You can use a keyboard shortcut to launch Help: simply press F1.

Click this icon:

under the Title bar to launch Index.

Using Index
Do the following:

| Type in the word you want to look up

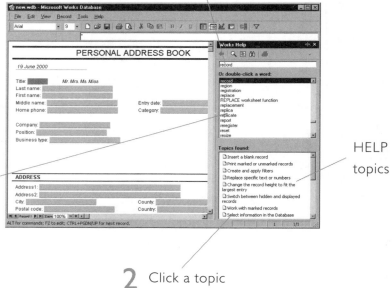

If typing in a keyword in step 1 does not produce a relevant topic, scroll through available headings here until you locate the right one, then double-click it and omit step 2.

(If you still can't find the right heading, follow the procedures on the facing page.)

HELP topics

2 Click a topic

To print out HELP information, click this button immediately below the Title bar:

View the relevant topic. Finally, carry out step 3:

3 When you've finished viewing the topic, click this button: ☒ in the upper right hand corner of the Index window to close it

Complete the Print dialog, then click OK.

Using the Answer Wizard

In any HELP window, click any link (coloured green) to display further information. In the example below, the highlighted phrase 'record number' is clicked (Before); the result is a useful definition (After).

If neither of the methods on pages 187-188 works, you can use another. You can type in Plain English questions. When you've done this, you can have Works search through its HELP database for relevant topics.

Asking questions with the Answer Wizard

From any Database HELP screen, perform steps 1-4:

1 If the Answer Wizard isn't already displaying, click this button just below the HELP screen's Title bar:

Before

2. Click the record number to select where you want to insert a blank record.

After

2. Click the record number (the row number to the left of each record in List view) to select where you want to insert a blank record.

2 Type in a question (e.g. 'How do I insert new records?') and click Search

3 Click the relevant topic heading

To close the Answer Wizard, follow step 3 on the facing page.

To print out HELP information, click this button immediately below the Title bar:

Complete the Print dialog, then click OK.

4 View the associated topic

Other ways to get assistance

There are more immediate ways to get help:

- moving the mouse pointer over Toolbar buttons produces an explanatory HELP bubble:

- Fields in dialogs have associated Help boxes. To view a box, first right-click in a field. Then carry out the following procedure:

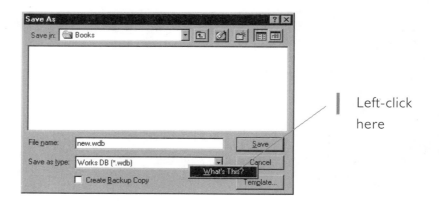

Left-click here

2 Works Suite 2000 now launches a HELP box:

Specifies the type of file you are saving.

Other standard Windows HELP features are also present; see your Windows documentation for how to use these.

The Calendar

This chapter gives you the basics of using the Calendar. You'll learn how to view specific dates; switch to different views; and insert appointments and events. You'll go on to make appointments and events recurring, set alarms and apply filters as a way of restricting which appointments/ events display. Finally, you'll discover how to track national/religious holidays, and print out your Calendar.

Covers

Chapter Five

The Calendar – an overview

To have Calendar display religious or national holidays, pull down the Edit menu and click Add Holidays. In the Add Holidays to Calendar dialog, select 1 or more countries. Click OK.

Here, Week view is recording a UK holiday

You can use the Calendar module to:

* track appointments

* track events

* track national holidays

* set alarms which remind you of important appointments/ events

* make appointments etc. recurring

Printing

To print the Calendar, pull down the File menu and click Print. Now do the following:

The Calendar module has in-built help. To use this, follow the instructions on pages 187-190.

| Click here; select a style

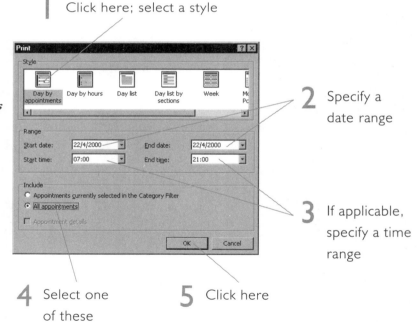

2 Specify a date range

3 If applicable, specify a time range

4 Select one of these

5 Click here

Re step 4 – select All appointments to print all appointments, OR Appointments currently selected in the Category Filter to print only pre-selected ones (see page 194).

6 Complete the 2nd Print dialog (for how to do this, see steps 3-6 on page 186) then click OK

The Calendar screen

Below is an illustration of the Calendar screen:

Here, the Calendar is displaying one day only, split into its component hours. This is called Day View.

(There are two other views. Week View shows a 7-day week, starting from Monday, while Month View shows every day in the given month.)

Title bar   Menu bar

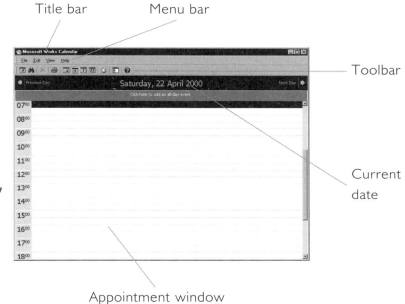

Toolbar

Current date

Appointment window

Re step 1 – you can also use an inbuilt calendar. Click the arrow to the right of the Enter date: field. Do the following:

A Click here to move back or forward a month

B Click here

Now perform step 2.

Jumping to dates

To view new dates, pull down the Edit menu and click Go To, Date. (Alternatively, press Ctrl+G.) Now do the following:

1 Enter a date

2 Click here

Entering appointments

In any Calendar view, double-click the day for which you want to enter the appointment. Do the following:

You can specify how many days the Calendar displays. Pull down the View menu and select Day, Week or Month.

To apply a category to your new appointment, click the Change button. In the dialog, select 1 or more categories. Click OK. Finally, perform step 5.

1 | Name the appointment

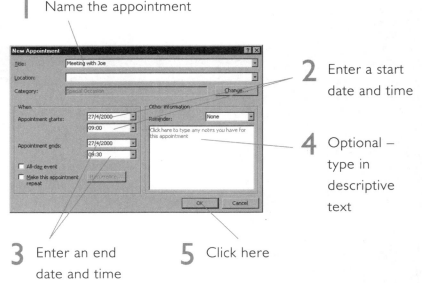

2 Enter a start date and time

4 Optional – type in descriptive text

3 Enter an end date and time

5 Click here

The Calendar lets you classify appointments. For example, if you apply a pre-defined category called 'Business' to all meetings you set up, you can have the Calendar display only those entries associated with the category. You do this by applying a filter.

Applying filters

Pull down the View menu and click Show Category Filter. Do the following:

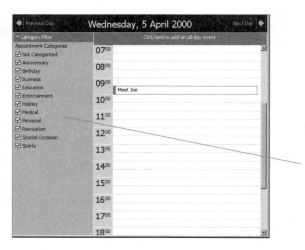

To view all appointments again, pull down the View menu and click Category Filter, Show appointments in all categories.

1 Deselect categories relating to appointments you don't want to view

Appointment management

To set up an alarm (either when you create an appointment, or when you edit it), click in this button:

In the list which launches, select a reminder option (e.g. '1 hour' or '1 week').

To make an appointment recurring (either when you create it or when you edit it), select Make this appointment repeat. Click this button:

Complete the Recurrence Options dialog (e.g. specify the period you want the recurrence to operate, and the frequency). Click OK.

The Calendar's in-build HELP system works like HELP in the Database and Spreadsheet modules.

You can perform various actions on appointments you've already set up.

Editing appointments

In any Calendar view, double-click an appointment. Carry out steps 1–4, as appropriate. Finally, perform step 5:

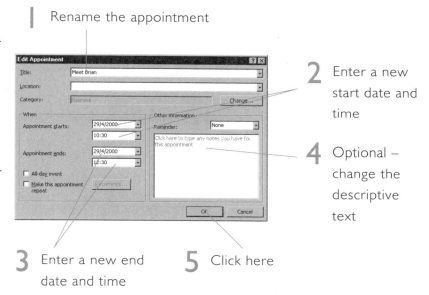

1 Rename the appointment

2 Enter a new start date and time

4 Optional – change the descriptive text

3 Enter a new end date and time

5 Click here

Moving appointments

First, launch the appropriate Calendar view. Place the mouse pointer over the relevant appointment. Hold down the left mouse button and drag it to a new date and/or time.

Deleting appointments

Right-click an appointment. In the menu, select Delete Item. Do the following:

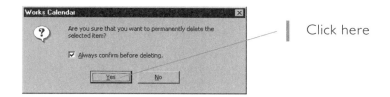

Click here

Entering events

The Calendar makes a distinction between appointments and events.

Appointments relate to a specific time (e.g. a meeting) while events either do not (e.g. a birthday) or are spread out over more than one day (e.g. holidays or conferences).

You can use the Calendar to track events – see the DON'T FORGET tip.

Creating an event

Select the relevant Calendar view and do the following:

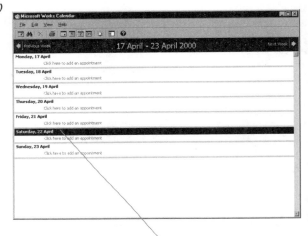

This is Week View. To select another view, see the HOT TIP on page 194.

To edit an existing event, double-click it in any view. Follow steps 1 - 5 (as appropriate) on page 195).

(Events can also be moved and deleted – follow the procedures under 'Moving appointments' and 'Deleting appointments' on page 195.)

To make the event recurring, or to apply an alarm, follow the procedures in the two HOT TIPS on page 195.

| Double-click the day you want the event to start on

2 Name the event   **3** Enter a start date

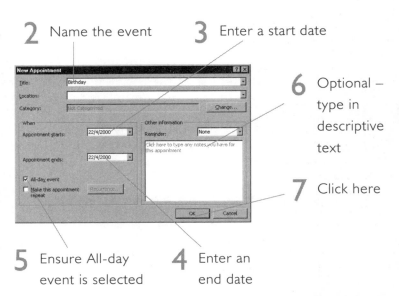

6 Optional – type in descriptive text

7 Click here

5 Ensure All-day event is selected   **4** Enter an end date

Home Publishing 2000

This chapter gives you the basics of using Home Publishing. You'll learn how to add text and pictures to projects you created in chapter 1, then you'll format the text appropriately and apply special effects to the images. Finally, you'll log on to the Home Publishing 2000 Web site for news and information; publish your completed projects to the Internet; send them via e-mail; and use built-in HELP.

Covers

Chapter Six

Customising your projects

For how to create blank projects, see pages 15-16. To create new projects based on templates, see the DON'T FORGET tip on page 18.

In chapter 1, we discussed how to create:

- blank projects

- template-based projects

In this chapter, we'll explore how to customise your new projects to best effect.

Adding text to template-based projects

Home Publishing templates come with text placeholders. These represent an easy and convenient way to add your own text. Do the following:

To add text to a blank project, click Add something, Text in the Main Options Command bar on the left of the Home screen (if you're not already here, press Ctrl+N). Home Publishing inserts a new text placeholder. Drag this to the correct location then follow step 2.

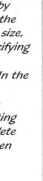

1 Click in a placeholder (notice that the Command bar on the left changes to Text Options)

You can format text (e.g. by changing the font/type size, or by specifying the alignment).
Right-click the text. In the menu, select Change formatting. In the sub-menu, select a formatting type (e.g. Font). Complete the resulting dialog, then click OK.

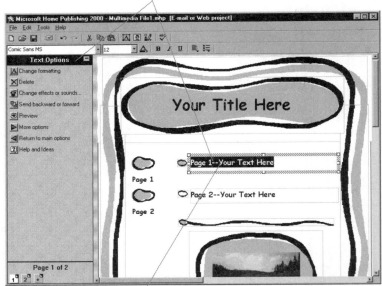

To spell-check your text, press F7. Complete the Check Spelling dialog (for guidelines on how to do this, see page 67).

2 Type in your own text then click outside the placeholder

Adding pictures

To add animations via the Clip Gallery, follow step 1. In the Gallery, ensure the Motion Clips tab is active. Now carry out standard procedures to select a clip category and insert a specific clip.

(Animations are static in paper-based projects.)

You can add pictures to projects

- via the Clip Gallery

- via a separate dialog

The Clip Gallery route

In a blank or template-generated project, do the following:

For help with working with projects, use Home Publishing's in-built HELP system.

- *To launch HELP, press F1.*

- *To find help for a topic, click the Index tab. Type in a keyword (e.g. 'pictures'), select a sub-topic (e.g. 'moving') then click Display. The specific HELP topic displays*

- *To work through a topic hierarchy, click the Contents tab. Click a heading (e.g. 'E-Mail and Web Projects') then a sub-heading (e.g. 'Publish to the Web'). The specific HELP topic displays*

1 Click Add something, Picture or animation from Clip Gallery

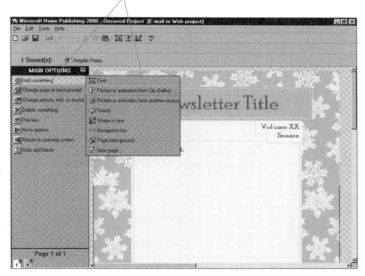

2 Use the Clip Gallery to insert a picture (by following steps 1-3 on page 71)

The dialog route

1 Follow step 1 above (but choose Add something, Picture or animation from another source, My computer)

2 Use the Select Picture or Animation File dialog to locate and select a picture file. Finally, click Open

Transforming pictures

If an effect isn't emphatic enough, repeat it as often as necessary.

You can apply a variety of effects to pictures.

Applying effects

First select the relevant picture by clicking it. Do the following:

Click Edit picture

To vary the magnification at which you view your projects, click Zoom in the Command Bar: In the menu, select a Zoom percentage (e.g. Page width or 150%).

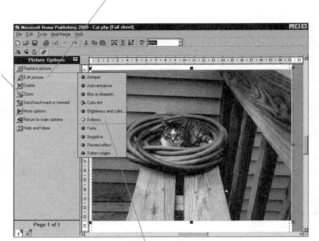

2 Select an effect (and, if necessary, complete any further dialog)

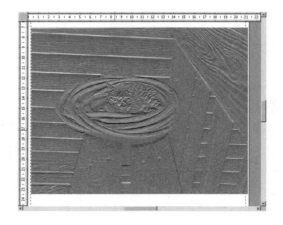

The image after the Emboss effect has been applied

Publishing projects on the Web

Any project you create can be published onto a Web site.

To update an existing Web site, open the amended project (see page 22 for how to do this). Follow steps 1-6 as appropriate.

Publishing your project

With your Internet connection live, pull down the File menu and click Publish to Web, Publish to a Web Site. Now:

1 Select 'As my home page' (to save your project as a complete Web site – the 1st page is the Home page) or 'As this folder within my site' (to save it as a linked folder)

Re step 1 – if you chose As this folder within my site also enter the folder name here:

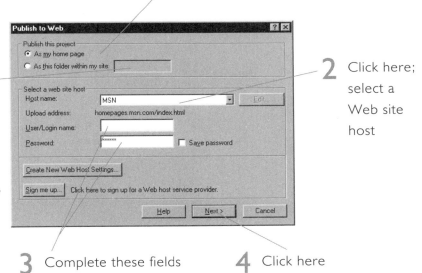

2 Click here; select a Web site host

Re step 2 – if you don't have a Web host, do the following before you complete the Publish to Web dialog.
With your Internet connection live, click Sign me up then follow the on-screen instructions.

3 Complete these fields

4 Click here

Re step 2 – if you already have a host but it isn't listed, do the following before you complete the Publish to Web dialog.
Click Create New Web Host Settings. Complete the resulting dialog (if you need help, consult your ISP). Click OK.

5 After step 4, Home Publishing converts your project to HTML format:

6 Home Publishing sends your project to your Web site host's server

Sending projects via e-mail

You can visit the dedicated Home Publishing Web site for:

- *news*
- *informational articles*
- *free downloads*

With your Internet connection live, pull down the Help menu and click Microsoft Home Publishing 2000 on the Web:

Click Home Publishing for further services

Re step 1 – select 'As an attachment in an e-mail message' to have your project included as a separate attachment (then follow the on-screen instructions).

If you want to send a signed copy of the e-mail, also complete the CC (Carbon Copy) section.

You can send your active project as an e-mail.

With your Internet connection live, pull down the File menu and click Send by E-mail. Now do the following:

1 Select your e-mail program

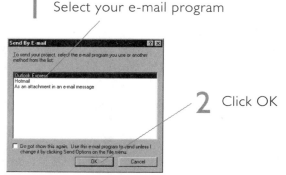

2 Click OK

3 Type in the recipient's e-mail address

4 Type in a subject

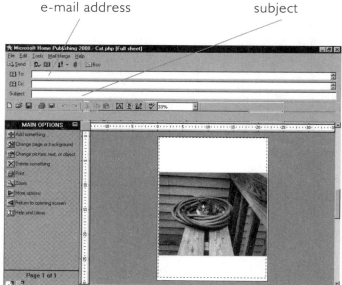

5 Click this toolbar button:

Encarta Interactive World Atlas 2000

This chapter gives you the basics of using Encarta Interactive World Atlas. You'll locate specific places and view them in the on-screen Map, then you'll manipulate it with the mouse and zoom in on the area you want. Next, you'll go on to customise how the Map displays. Finally, you'll activate place-specific Web links, to enrich your use of Encarta Interactive World Atlas, and use the on-board HELP system.

Covers

Chapter Seven

Finding places

If you're not used to using electronic atlases, you might wish to run the Encarta World Atlas product tour.
In the Home screen, click Product Tour then follow the on-screen instructions.

You can use a dedicated Find dialog (called the Pinpointer) to locate and view specific places in the Atlas Map:

1 From within any World Atlas view, press Ctrl+F

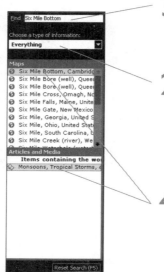

3 Type in a place name

Re step 4 – sometimes the Pinpointer also provides direct access to Web links relating to the place specified in step 3. Click the entry e.g.:

London, Web Links

then follow the instructions on page 208.

2 Optional – click here and select an information category (e.g. Countries) to limit the search

4 Click the correct place entry or an informational article/picture

You can view information on related areas. For example, as Six Mile Bottom is in Cambridge-shire, you can choose to view the county map.
Position the mouse pointer over the place name then left-click. Do the following:

The Atlas displays the selected place entry (as here) or article/picture

Make the relevant selections

5 To close the Pinpointer, press Ctrl+F again

Using the Map

To return to the Home screen at any time, refer to the overhead toolbar and click this button:

On the facing page we saw how using the Pinpointer produces a highly tailored map. You can customise this map in a variety of ways.

Moving the Map

To reposition the Map focus, refer to the toolbar at the base of the Map screen. Do the following:

Encarta World Atlas comes with in-built HELP. To activate this, press F1. Then:

- *To find help for a topic, click the Index tab. Type in details (e.g. 'product tour') then double-click the relevant heading below. The specific topic displays*

- *To work through a topic hierarchy, click the Contents tab. Click a heading (e.g. 'Learn about the map') then a sub-heading. The specific HELP topic displays*

Click here

In the example below, the emphasis of the view has been changed to favour Europe:

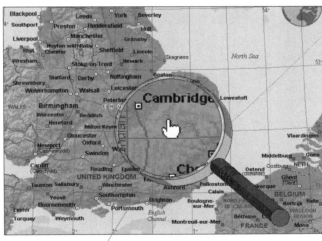

2 Place the mouse pointer over the Map; drag to move the view

Zooming in on the Map

To increase or decrease the Map magnification, do the following:

To view articles relating to the place currently being viewed in the Map, click the following button:

Articles and Media

Now click the relevant entry in the drop-down menu e.g.:

Facts and Figures

The illustration below shows a sample article:

1 In the toolbar at the base of the screen, click this button:

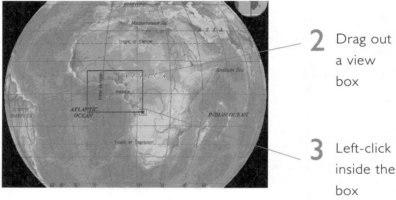

2 Drag out a view box

3 Left-click inside the box

4 Encarta Interactive World Atlas magnifies the area within the box:

Customising the Map

If the left-hand panel isn't fully displaying, refer to the top left of the Map screen and click this button:

You can customise how the Map displays in two ways:

- by specifying an overall map style

- by specifying which map components display

Applying a new style

| In the panel on the left of the screen, click this button:

The illustration below shows the effect of applying the Political style to the lower Map view on the facing page:

2 Select a Map style

Specifying Map components

| In the panel on the left of the screen, click this button:

Cartographer

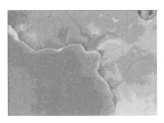

The illustration below shows the effect of removing all cartographic features from the lower Map view on the facing page:

2 Select or deselect the relevant components

Using Web links

If the Web Links button isn't visible, you may have to click this button first:

Articles and Media

When you've located a place with the Encarta Interactive World Atlas, you can have links to related Web sites display.

First, ensure your Internet connection is live. Then:

In the panel on the left of the screen, click this button:

Web Links

You can use the Map to have associated pictures display.
Click this button in the left-hand panel:

Multimedia Map

Move the mouse pointer over a specific location on the Map. Small pictures appear e.g.:

2 Click here

Click a picture; the full-size image launches in a dedicated viewer.

3 Activate a link

If you're connected to the Internet via an Internet Service Provider, remember to close your connection before returning to Encarta World Atlas.

4 Activate any further links, as necessary

Money 2000

This chapter gives you the basics of using Money 2000. You'll create and use your own accounts, then enter and classify transactions. You'll also edit existing transactions; create your own categories/sub-categories; and set up your accounts for on-line services. Finally, you'll use the on-line HELP system; view your account data as reports/charts; balance your accounts; and print out transaction or category details.

Covers

Chapter Eight

Using accounts

Some basic terminology

Money 2000 organises your finances in accounts. Accounts are collections of associated transactions (withdrawals or deposits). Transactions are entered into accounts via the Account Register (which, for ease of use, resembles a cheque book).

You can set up accounts for online services (e.g. for downloading account statements or share quotes). To do this, press Ctrl+Shift+A. On the left of the screen, select Set up accounts. Click Set up online services in the main screen, then select an account from the list. Finally, click Set Up and follow the on-screen instructions.

Many users find they only need the default account created by Money 2000; others, on the other hand, discover that as they become more proficient there is a need to create further accounts. A common example would be the user who needs to utilise Money to manage his domestic affairs and a small business. In this situation, having separate accounts for both makes a lot of sense. You don't *need* to do this – you can use categories (see later) to differentiate perfectly adequately between transaction types – but it is both logical and convenient.

Money makes creating further accounts easy.

Other reasons for creating new accounts are:

If your bank does not let you use online services directly from Money, visit its Web site. You may well be able to:

- view account data, and/or;
- download statements

- to handle individual businesses separately

- to handle petty cash transactions separately

There are various types of accounts, but the procedures for creating them are basically identical.

Money provides a convenient base from which to work with accounts: the Account Manager. (See the facing page for more information.)

You should backup your account data regularly. To do this, pull down the File menu and click Back Up. Follow the on-screen instructions.

Creating accounts

Money 2000 provides a special Wizard to help you create new accounts. The New Account Wizard leads you by the hand through the process of account creation, asking all the questions which need to be answered.

Using the New Account Wizard

If applicable, ensure you have your chequebook or Building Society passbook to hand. Then press Ctrl+Shift+A . Carry out the following steps:

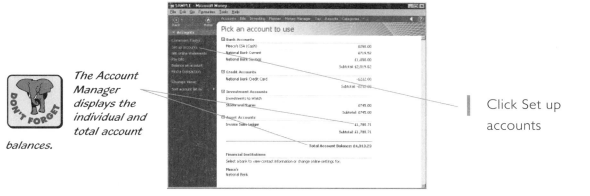

The Account Manager displays the individual and total account balances.

Click Set up accounts

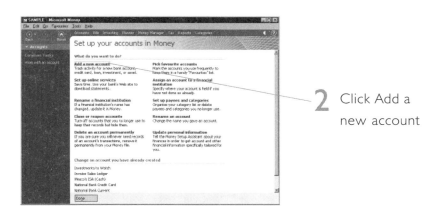

Click Add a new account

3 Complete the wizard dialogs – click Next to move on to successive dialogs, and Finish to complete the process

Transactions – an overview

The following points are central to the way Money works:

- Money defines a transaction as anything which affects the balance of an account

You can enter information directly into the Register, or via the form (an add-on which appears by default and makes data entry even easier).
(This book demonstrates the form method.)

- you enter transactions directly into the Register, a special window which lets you access the account

- within the account, transactions are entered into *fields.* The main fields are:

    — Num

    — Date

    — Payee

    — Payment

    — Deposit

    — Balance

    — Pay to or From

    — Category/Subcategory

    — Memo

Money 2000 comes with in-built HELP. To activate this, press F1. Then:

- *To find help for a topic, click 🏮 in the overhead toolbar. Type in details (e.g. 'transaction') then press Enter. Double-click the relevant heading (e.g. 'Assign a category to a transaction') below. The specific topic displays*

- *To work through a topic hierarchy, click 📄 in the overhead toolbar. Click a heading (e.g. 'Online'). Repeat until the specific HELP topic displays*

Transaction types

Transactions fall into various types. The principal ones are:

- Deposit

- Transfer

- Withdrawal

Entering transactions

To open an account (prior to entering transactions), refer to the Account Manager and do the following:

🗇 **Bank Accounts**

Mesco's ISA (Cash)

Click an account entry

Re step 1 – this creates a new transaction. If you want to amend an existing one instead, highlight it in the Register and click the Edit button instead. Now carry out steps 3-4.

Some transactions benefit from being 'split'. For instance, if you send an insurance company a cheque for £569.50 which relates to more than 1 premium, it's useful to show the make-up in your accounts (e.g. 'Motor £445.00, House £124.50).

You split transactions by applying a separate category to each component. To do this, click the Split button, then complete the resulting dialog. Click Done when you've finished.

Entering data into accounts is easy. Carry out the following steps to create a new transaction:

Fields

The Register

The data entry form

Click New

2 Click a transaction tab (select Transfer if you need to transfer money from one Money account to another)

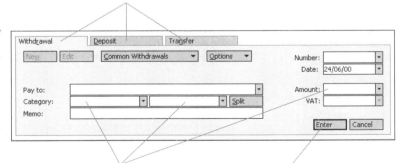

3 Complete the relevant fields (see page 215 for how to complete the Category field)

4 Click here

Categories – an overview

Traditional book-based accounts make use of identifying headings – for instance, outgoings are entered as 'Stationery' or 'Drawings'. Money takes this practice and extends it almost infinitely, and with much more detail. It does this by allowing you to assign 'categories' to transactions.

Categories fall into two main divisions: Income (applied to deposits) or Expense (applied to withdrawals).

Categories are convenient labels; you can – and should – use them to:

- organise your accounts and make them much more detailed

- produce tailor-made reports – see pages 216-217

- produce customised graphs – see pages 216-217

Limiting reports or graphs to specific categories produces a much more precise result.

Sub-categories

To ensure even greater precision, categories can – and very often are – divided into sub-categories. For example, the Expense category 'Pet Care' is split into:

- Food

- Pet Insurance

- Supplies

- Vet's Bills

Differentiation

Money differentiates between categories and sub-categories by placing them in separate fields:

Category and Sub-category fields in the Register form

Creating categories

As we've seen, when you allocate categories and/or sub-categories to your transactions, you can select from numerous ready-made choices which cover most conceivable situations. In the early stages of your use of Money, this will certainly be sufficient. As your experience increases, however, you'll probably want to create your own. Creating categories and sub-categories is easy and convenient.

Creating a new category

In the course of entering a new transaction or amending an existing one, do the following:

To create a sub-category, first ensure the correct category is displaying in the Category field. Click in the Sub-category field. In the drop-down list, select Add a New Subcategory. Complete the dialog which launches and click Next. Complete the second dialog and click Finish – Money 2000 adds the new sub-category to the Categories list:

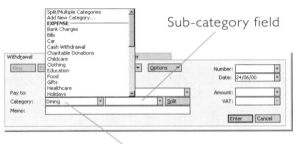

Sub-category field

New sub-category

1 Click in the Category field, type in a name for the new category then press Enter

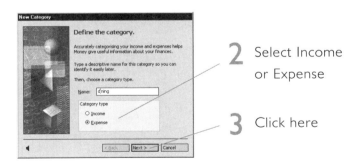

2 Select Income or Expense

3 Click here

4 Complete the remaining dialog, then click Finish

Reports and charts – an overview

All accounts should be 'balanced' (balancing – more formally known as 'reconciliation' – is the process of:

- *transposing bank statement information (for example, bank charges and interest payments) into the corresponding Money account*

- *comparing the bank statement with the account and marking as 'reconciled' those transactions which are identical in both*

- *totalling the number of cleared items in both the statement and account, and making sure the two totals tally, and;*

- *resolving any instances where the statement and account don't tally*

For help with balancing your accounts, press Ctrl+Shift+A. On the left of the screen, select Balance an account. Press F1. In Money 2000's HELP window, click a topic e.g.:

☐ Balance (reconcile) a bank or loan account to a paper statement

Now follow the on-screen instructions.

Money makes managing your day-to-day finances easy. However, it's also vital to be able to take an overview of them. You can do this in two ways:

- verbally, by generating reports

- visually, by generating charts

Use Money's report formats to achieve a detailed written evaluation of your finances, based on the heading you select. Utilise its charting capability to make a similar kind of evaluation *instantly*. Better still, use both reports and charts for a comprehensive picture of how your finances are progressing.

A sample report

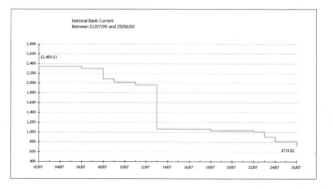

A sample chart

Creating a standard report/chart

You can customise exactly how a given report or chart displays. For example, you can specify:

- *which accounts it applies to*
- *which transaction types are featured*
- *which dates it applies to*
- *which categories are featured*
- *which font and/or type size is used*
- *which fields are included, and;*
- *(if applicable) the chart type*

To customise a report or chart, click the Customise button before or after creation. Now complete the resulting dialog. Click OK to regenerate the report/chart.

To print out reports or charts, carry out steps 1-2 on page 218.

To have Money 2000 compile a report or chart for you, press Ctrl+Shift+R . Carry out the following steps:

Click here

3 Click here

2 Click here

The completed report

Print options

Before you start printing, you should specify the relevant print setup options. These include:

- *ensuring the correct printer is selected*
- *specifying the page orientation (landscape or portrait), and;*
- *specifying the page size*

To do any of these, pull down the File menu and click Print Setup, Report and Chart Setup. Complete the resulting dialog, then click OK.

Money lets you print out details of current transactions. You do this by printing the contents of the active account (but not the screen itself). You can also print category lists. This is especially useful when the number of categories you use is large; it can sometimes be preferable to refer to a printed list to find the one you want to use than to scroll through the on-screen Category drop-down list.

Printing the Account Register contents

Within the Register, press Ctrl+P. Do the following:

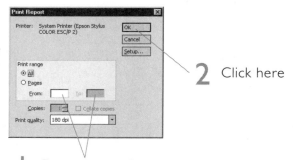

2 Click here

Enter start and end page numbers, if appropriate

Printing lists

Press Ctrl+Shift+C. Do the following:

You can also print out a list of payees. Simply click Payees here then press Ctrl+P and follow steps 1 and 2 above.

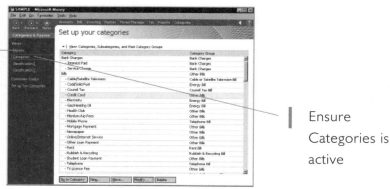

Ensure Categories is active

Now press Ctrl+P and follow steps 1 and 2 above.

AutoRoute Express 2000

This chapter gives you the basics of using AutoRoute Express 2000. You'll create a route (setting start and end locations and – optionally – intervening stops) then save it to disk. Next, you'll locate specific places and view them in the on-screen Map then go on to customise how the Map displays. Finally, you'll activate place-specific Web links, to enrich your use of AutoRoute Express 2000, and use the on-board HELP system.

Covers

Chapter Nine

Planning a trip

You can use AutoRoute Express 2000 to:

- plan routes (specifying the start and end destinations and a variety of additional variables)

- locate places you're interested in

- save calculated routes for later use

Route planning

To plan a route after you've started AutoRoute Express 2000, omit steps 1-2. Press Ctrl+N to clear any active route, then Ctrl+R. Now carry out steps 3-7.

You can customise a host of route variables – for example, you can specify:

- *whether AutoRoute Express 2000 calculates the quickest, shortest or the most scenic route (these settings can be applied to trip sections)*

- *driving speeds and the length of the driving day*

- *fuel consumption settings, and/or;*

- *fuel costs*

To do this, click the Trip Options button before you carry out step 7. Now complete the Trip Options dialog. When you've finished, click OK.

Just after starting AutoRoute Express 2000, do the following:

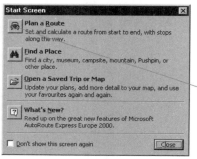

2 Click here

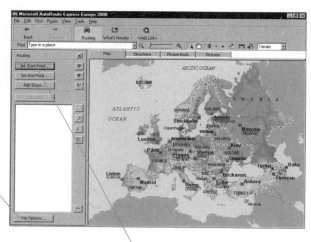

3 Click Set Start Point

4 Type in the start name and press Enter

If you want to specify any intervening stops, click Add Stops
immediately after performing step 6. Type in the name of a stop and press Enter. In the list which appears, double-click the correct entry.

Repeat this for as many stops as you want to insert.

5 Double-click the correct place entry

6 Repeat steps 3-5 to set the destination. In step 3, however, select Set End Point; in steps 4-5, select a destination

You can have the Overview Map display. This shows the area currently
being viewed in overall context:

7 Click this button:

Route details

To launch (or close) the Overview Map, pull down the Tools menu and click Overview Map.

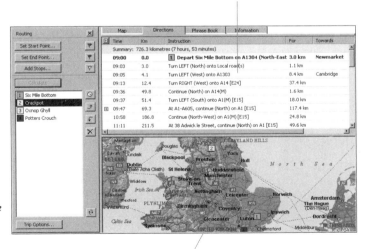

The route as a map

Saving routes

You can save calculated routes for later use.

Saving your trip

Pull down the File menu and click Save As. Now do the following:

Re step 1 on the immediate right – you may have to double-click one or more folders first, to locate the folder you want to host the route.

To print out the active route/ map, press Ctrl+P. Complete the Print dialog, then click OK.

Click here; in the list, select a drive

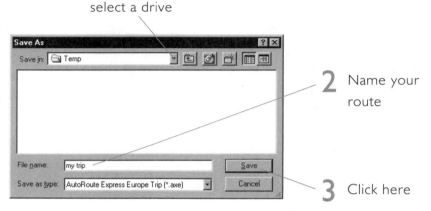

2 Name your route

3 Click here

Opening routes

Pull down the File menu and click Open. Now do the following:

Re step 1 on the immediate right – you may have to double-click one or more folders first, to locate the folder containing the relevant route.

Click here; in the list, select a drive

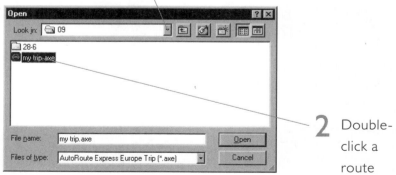

2 Double-click a route

Finding places

When you've located a place, you can connect to the Internet and view sites related to it.

With your connection live, click this button in the toolbar:

A dialog launches – click OK. In the resultant screen, click a link e.g.:

🌐 The best of the web on Yarmouth

In the next screen, click a precise link e.g.:

TRAVEL   Isle of Wight Council
            Government and business information for the Isle of Wight

You can use a dedicated Find dialog to locate and view specific places:

1 │ Press Ctrl+F

2 Type in the place you want to find

3 Double-click the correct place entry

The selected place entry displays

As here, you can view a list of sites (e.g. airports, golf courses, museums and galleries) related to the place currently being viewed.

Click this button in the toolbar:

(To specify which sites display, click Preferences. In the Preferences dialog, deselect those sites you don't wish to view. Click OK.)

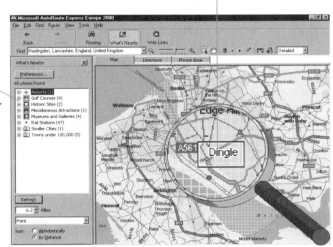

Using the Map

AutoRoute Express 2000 comes with in-built HELP. To activate this, press F1. Then:

- *To find help for a topic, click the Index tab. Type in details (e.g. 'route') then double-click the relevant heading below. The specific topic displays*

- *To work through a topic hierarchy, click the Contents tab. Double-click a heading (e.g. 'Navigating the map') then a sub-heading. The specific HELP topic displays*

On page 223, we saw how using the Find dialog produces a highly tailored map. You can customise this map in a variety of ways.

Moving the Map

To reposition the Map focus, refer to the toolbar at the top of the Map screen. Do the following:

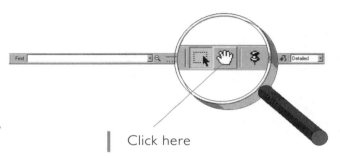

Click here

In the example below, the Map focus has been moved to the right:

You can change the Map format. Simply press Ctrl+M repeatedly to cycle through available options (Simple, Detailed, Terrain and Political).

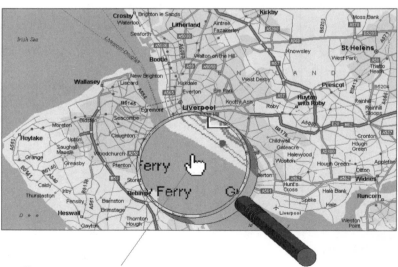

2 Place the mouse pointer over the Map; drag to move the view

Picture It! Express 2000

This chapter gives you the basics of using Picture It! Express 2000. You'll learn how to add text to pictures you created in chapter 1, then you'll edit/resize the text appropriately and apply special effects to the images. Finally, you'll log on to the Picture It! Web site, send your pictures via e-mail and use the built-in HELP.

Covers

Chapter Ten

Working with pictures

For how to create blank pictures, see page 16. To create new pictures based on templates, see the HOT TIP on page 18.

Once you've created a new picture in Picture It! Express 2000 (or opened an existing one) you can:

- add text

- apply a variety of special effects

Adding text

Do the following in the Picture It! Express 2000 screen:

1 Click Text, Add Text

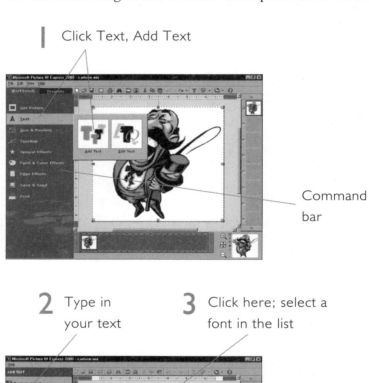

Command bar

To move the new text at any time, place the mouse pointer over the text frame – it turns into a hand:

Text frame

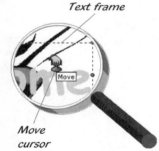

Move cursor

Drag the text frame to a new location:

2 Type in your text

3 Click here; select a font in the list

4 Select a colour

5 Click Done

Brightness/contrast adjustment

To edit existing text, select the relevant frame. Under the Workbench tab in the Command bar, select Text, Edit Text. Now follow steps 2-4 (as appropriate) on the facing page. Finally, follow step 5.

Adjusting brightness/contrast

Do the following in the Picture It! Express 2000 screen:

1 Click Touchup under the Workbench tab in the Command bar. In the graphical menu, select Brightness & Contrast

To amend text size, first select the relevant frame. Place the mouse pointer over one of the corner handles — it changes to:

Drag the handle outwards to increase the size or inwards to decrease it.

2 Drag one or both of these sliders

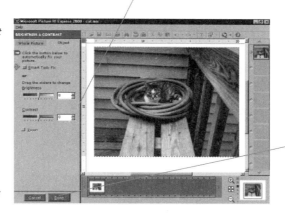

3 Click Done

To remove 'red-eye' (an undesirable effect in photography when light from the flash is reflected from the subject's retina on to the film, producing a red colour) follow step 1 but select Fix Red Eye in the graphical menu. Click within the eye and select:

Repeat for each eye then click Done.

Here, both brightness and contrast have been increased

Focus adjustment

Sharpening/blurring pictures

Do the following in the Picture It! Express 2000 screen:

Repeat or combine special effects for added impact.

1 Click Special Effects under the Workbench tab in the Command bar. In the menu, select Blur or Sharpen Focus

2 Drag this slider to the left (Blur) or right (Sharpen)

3 Click Done

This is the same image with maximum sharpness:

Here, maximum blur has been applied

Using Picture Putty

Using automatic distortion
Do the following in the Picture It! Express 2000 screen:

1 Click Special Effects under the Workbench tab in the Command bar. In the menu, select Picture Putty

To distort manually, do the following. In step 2, click this button instead:

2 Click this button:

In the Command bar on the left of the screen:

- *select a distortion type, and;*
- *select a brush ('ball') size*

Now place the mouse pointer where you want the distortion to begin. Hold down the mouse button and drag repeatedly over the picture. Release the button. Finally, click Done.

3 Select a distortion

4 Drag the slider to specify the extent of the distortion

5 Click Done

'Smear' has been applied manually

This is the Twirl distortion set to '40'

Converting to black-and-white

Making pictures monochrome

Do the following in the Picture It! Express 2000 screen:

1 Click Paint & Color Effects, Black and White

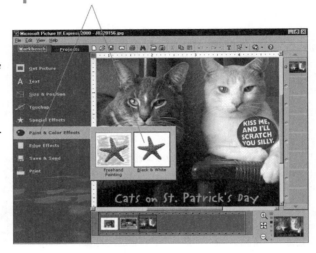

To paint pictures, do the following. In step 1, select Freehand Painting instead. In the Command bar on the left of the screen:

- *select a paint tool*
- *select a paint colour, and;*
- *select a brush ('ball') size*

Now place the mouse pointer where you want to start painting. Hold down the mouse button and drag over the picture. Repeat this as often as necessary, then release the button.

Finally, click Done.

A tick has been painted in

2 Click here

3 Click Done

Softening edges

1 Click Edge Effects under the Workbench tab in the Command bar. In the graphical menu, select Soft Edges

To remove scratches from the active picture, click Touchup, Remove Scratch under the Workbench tab in the Command bar on the left of the screen. Select a brush ('ball') size then click along the length of the scratch (if you need help with this, click Show me how then follow the on-screen instructions).
  Repeat for any further scratches, then click Done.

2 Use this slider to set the degree of softening

3 Click Done

To change a picture's tint, click Touchup, Correct Tint under the Workbench tab in the Command bar on the left of the screen. Drag the ball on the coloured ring until you reach the correct colour, then do the following:

Drag this to the correct setting

Click Done when you've finished.

Here, maximum softening has been applied

Sending pictures via e-mail

You can visit the dedicated Picture It! Express 2000 Web site.

With your Internet connection live, pull down the Help menu and click Microsoft on the Web, Microsoft Picture It! Express Home Page. This is the result:

Click Done to return to your picture

You can send your active project as an e-mail.

With your Internet connection live, click Edge Effects under the Workbench tab in the Command bar. In the graphical menu, select Soft Edges. Now do the following:

1 Click Save & Send, Send or Save for E-mail

2 Select a size

For help with working with pictures, use the in-built HELP:

- *To launch HELP, press F1.*

- *To find help for a topic, click the Index tab. Type in a keyword. Select a sub-topic then click Display. The specific HELP topic displays*

- *To work through a topic hierarchy, click the Contents tab. Click one or more headings then the relevant sub-heading. The specific HELP topic displays*

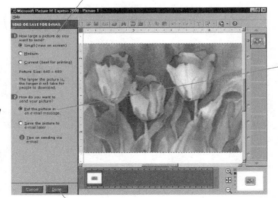

3 Select Put the picture in an e-mail message

4 Click Done

5 Carry out any additional on-screen instructions

Index

D

T